The Good Samaritan

Fred Baker

Grade 2

HELPING
CHILDREN
WORSHIP

Catherine Herzel

Philip R. Hoh, editor

LCA Leadership Education Series

© 1963, by the Lutheran
Church Press, Philadelphia,
Pa. Printed in the United
States of America
9993L63   LB537

CONTENTS

Chapter 1 **The Nature of Worship** . . . 9

Chapter 2 **The Child at Worship** . . . 23

Chapter 3 **Unplanned Worship** . . . 36

Chapter 4 **Planned Worship** . . . 45

Chapter 5 **Instruction in Worship** . . . 64

Chapter 6 **Resources for Worship** . . . 90

Appendix A . . . 135

Appendix B . . . 138

AGE RANGE

This book and its leadership course are primarily for teachers and leaders of children of grade school age (6-12).

Some mention is made of three-, four-, and five-year-olds, because one of the new hymnals is designed for the pre-reading child and because there will not be a separate course on worship for these younger children. There are sections on worship in both *Bible and Doctrine for 3's to 5's*, and *Ways to Teach 3's to 5's*.

ART

The art for this book was done by children attending church schools at Zion Lutheran Church, Flourtown, Pa., and Christ Lutheran Church, Oreland, Pa.

The children ranged from six to twelve years of age. They were told to use only two colors, so that their art could be reproduced with reasonable accuracy in this two-color printing. Their teachers gave a minimum of help; the ideas and the execution are those of the children.

Several hundred children participated. We regret that we have only enough space for a few of their artistic efforts. We didn't pick the best or the worst, chiefly because we didn't know which were which. We tried to select those which we thought would convey to the reader what the child was trying to put on paper.

DEFINITION OF WORSHIP

Worship is man's reverent response to a power vastly superior to himself.

Christian worship is man's reverent response to God as revealed in Christ.

Christian worship differs from all other forms because it is based on God, who comes to us and reveals himself. God makes our worship possible.

Defined simply on the basis of logic and conventional word usage, it is man who worships—though God has made this possible. Defined in a broader way, worship becomes a relationship between God and man, a communion.

Of all Christians, Lutherans are usually most concerned that God be given all the credit; his is the power and the glory. Sometimes, therefore, we give the impression that man can do nothing. Of course, he can in no way win his own salvation, nor can he climb to God by any sort of ladder. He is always utterly dependent upon God to take the initiative and provide the means—even to provide for faith.

But man has been given a measure of free will; he has the ability to make some choices. God never forces a man to worship him. We men may choose to worship or not to worship.

When a son has a wonderful father and shows his father respect and love, surely the son should receive no credit for doing so. This is part of being a son. This is expected. When we worship God, who is so wonderful to us, we can have no pride in our worship, no thought of reaping a reward. It is the right and salutary thing to do.

7

"Let the amen sound from his people again"

Yogi—Grade 6

1

The Nature of Worship

ONE afternoon Jake Barnes went into a church and began to pray. "I . . . prayed for everybody I thought of . . . then I prayed for myself again, and while I was praying for myself I found I was getting sleepy . . . So I prayed that I would make a lot of money, then I started to think how I would make it, and thinking of money reminded me of the Count, and I started wondering where he was, and regretting I hadn't seen him, and about something funny Brett had told me about him, and as all the time I was kneeling with my forehead on the wood in front of me, and was thinking of myself as praying, I was a little ashamed . . . I only wished I felt religious and maybe I would the next time."[1]

Brother Lawrence, a monk who lived in Lorraine in the seventeenth century, considered himself "a great awkward fellow who broke everything." When he entered a monastery he was assigned work in the kitchen, work which he did not particularly enjoy. Nevertheless, "the time of business does not with me differ from the time of prayer," he said, "and in the noise and clatter of my kitchen, while several persons are at the same time calling for different things, I possess God in as great tranquility as if I were upon my knees at the blessed sacrament."[2]

[1]Ernest Hemingway, *The Sun Also Rises* (New York: Charles Scribner's Sons, 1926), p. 97. Used by permission.
[2]Brother Lawrence, *The Practice of the Presence of God* (New York: Morehouse-Barlow, 1923).

Most of us share the worship experiences of both these men. Many times, like Jake Barnes, we go through the motions of worship without really worshiping. But sometimes our consciousness of God's presence is as vivid as that of Brother Lawrence. What makes the difference? Why is not our sense of worship always as sharp as that of Brother Lawrence?

Obstacles to worship

Sometimes we cannot worship God because we have raised personal barriers against worship. A woman who had been very active in her church began to drift away from its worship services. "Every time I come into the church and see that woman," she said, speaking of another church member, "I think of what she has done to me." Her resentment of another person rose up like thick fog to shut off all communication with God.

Jesus knew that our relationships with other people affect our relationship with God. He said, "If you are offering your gift at the altar, and there remember that your brother has something against you, leave your gift there before the altar and go; first be reconciled to your brother, and then come and offer your gift" *(Matthew 5:23, 24)*.

Sometimes our spirit of worship is smothered by the preoccupations we bring with us to church. Worry over our job, concern with the way we look, an avid interest in our neighbors—these, if we cannot put them aside, will effectively consume our time at worship and our receptivity to God's message.

Sometimes our expectations of worship are unreasonable. Parents know that there are wonderful moments when the tie with their children is close and expressive. A child says "I love you," and flings his arms around his parent's neck. These moments are all too unusual. Most of the parent-child relationship is carried on in more ordinary ways. Parents express their love for their child in ways that both child and parents take for granted. They see that he has warm clothes to wear, proper food to eat, that he learns to behave in a way that will accommodate to society. The analogy between parent and child and the worshiper and God is not a perfect one, but it does point out some truths. Human beings cannot seem to stay on an exalted plane of worship, though there are shining moments. We must accept our ordinariness and know that the commonplace worship has its value too, rejoicing in those rare moments when we are especially conscious of God's presence, but also accepting him as a steady influence on our lives.

Not only are our expectations often unreasonable, but we humans also have varying temperaments. The way of the mystic may not be our way of worshiping. To return to the analogy of parent and child, some children are not naturally demonstrative. A son may be leaving to go to the other end of the earth, but for him a firm handshake indicates very real love. Another son, in similar circumstances, would throw his arms around his parents and express his feelings in a flow of tender words. So it is that some of us find it easier to show our worship of God than others do. The less expressive person may not demonstrate his devotion by fervent prayer and joyful singing. We cannot expect our mode of worship to conform to that of any other individual. Each worships God in his own particular way.

This means that some forms of worship will be more appropriate to us than other forms. It means that some events will be more inspirational than others. It also means that going through the motions of worship does not guarantee worship. At certain times of our life one form of worship may appeal, and a few days or years later, a different mode of worship may seem more natural.

Two truths

When, at times, our worship seems empty, we should remember two truths. The first is that worship is based on the presence of God. He is there and he is real, no matter how fugitive our impulse to worship. The second truth is that God is constantly seeking us. Therefore, our worship will consist more of being found by God than seeking him ourselves. Quietness and confidence can be our strength.

Think about the liturgy of the church and you see that in the service of worship we celebrate God's seeking of us. Congregation and minister both proclaim God's seeking man through Christ. Again and again we sing and say our praise and thanks to God for the Son who came looking for us. Our own uneven feelings about worship seem less restricting when we accept the truth that God is active in our life.

Perhaps the greatest obstacle to our worship is that we do not rightly understand what worship is.

Worship has variety

When you went to church one particular Sunday morning, something wonderful happened. During that brief hour you reached out with a feeling of the greatness of God and you faced your own littleness and shortcomings. You came out of church feeling different than when you went in. You felt clean and good. You felt healthier and happier and secure in God's family. You had worshiped.

But worship includes other experiences, too. Do not be disappointed if that does not happen at every service.

Perhaps you were reading the Bible and the brightness of God's goodness came to you like a light turned on in a dark room. Or alone on a walk one afternoon you were pierced with a realization that God knew all your thoughts and deeds and nevertheless loved you very much. Then you walked on and thought about something altogether different. You had worshiped. But worship takes still other forms. It is more than that.

Worship may be compared to a great cathedral whose splendor we can never see all at one time. From a distance we may note the general outline of the building. We can walk all around the church and see many parts of it from many angles. But when we come close enough to observe the fine detail of the doors, then we cannot see the tower. And it will take many visits to the interior of the church before we realize its wealth of beauty.

In the same way, worship is a reality bigger than any single experience of it. We can only know it part by part and realize that we have had but glimpses of its tremendous vistas and majestic heights, its infinite detail, its divine beauty. This is natural, for the object of our worship is God, who is far beyond our understanding, who is both the Known and the Unknown, the Revealed and the Mysterious.

Worship is a relationship with God

It is easy to fall into the mistake of thinking of worship as something we go through, a cluster of words we say, traditional actions we perform. In the days of the prophet Amos, the children of Israel made this mistake. They understood worship to be the gatherings in the Temple, or the offerings on the altar, or the songs, or the ritual, matters which had little to do with the way they treated other people or their ideas about themselves and their relation to God. Amos thundered at them the word of God, "I hate, I despise your feasts. . . . Even though you offer me your burnt offerings and cereal offerings, I will not accept them; . . . to the melody of your harps I will not listen" *(Amos 5:21-23)*. The show of ritual performance was no substitute for worship. Worship was a live relationship between living individuals—men and God.

13

Our songs, our offerings, our gathering together in church are all vehicles for worship, but unless these vehicles carry a living relationship of the self with God, they are empty forms. Whether we are at a solemn celebration of the Holy Communion or bowing our heads in thanksgiving at a family breakfast, we are worshiping only when we are relating ourselves to God, or more accurately, when we are conscious that God is relating himself to us.

Worship begins when God reaches out to us and we respond to his love by reaching toward him. The parish education symbol on the jacket of this book could be a symbol for worship. The interlacing arms of God reaching down and man reaching up express the essence of worship (as well as parish education). The times when we are conscious of worship are like islands rising above the sea of everyday living. Underneath the waters of the sea, the islands flow into the earth and are linked in one continuous mass. Just so, our basic relationship with God must underlie every moment of our life, on occasion lifting above the waters and tides of living. But these high points are built on a foundation which links them and provides a stable base for all things. Our daily lives—every moment of them—are lived in relationship to God. All is worship, just as all is vocation and all is stewardship. Our conscious proclamations of God's lordship are high moments of worship, but all living is worship for those who are related to God. So we can say that worship is our total life responding to God. In general use, however, we tend to speak of worship as our conscious response to him.

Note again that worship does not originate with us. We respond to God because he is a God whose nature and character lead to adoration. God speaks to us first through his Word revealed in the Bible and proclaimed by his church. We reply in adoration, praise, contrition, thanksgiving, dedication, and service.

14

Worship is recognition of God's supreme worth

The prophet Isaiah was at worship in the Temple. Suddenly he was overwhelmed with a sense of the great purity and holiness of the Lord.

Holy, holy, holy is the Lord of hosts;
the whole earth is full of his glory (Isaiah 6:3)

The foundations of the Temple seemed to shake; Isaiah felt as if his whole life had been suddenly jarred loose from his old ways. He knew something of the nature of God and the knowledge was awesome. Isaiah worshiped him.

The apostle Peter saw the absolute goodness and purity of Jesus, and that glow showed up all the littleness and ugliness of his own life. He fell on his knees and said, "Depart from me, for I am a sinful man, O Lord." Peter recognized the supreme worth of Jesus. Peter worshiped him.

Our worship is a recognition of the superlatives of God. Look at some of the words we use in our morning service: "Almighty," "most merciful," "thine infinite mercy," "thou only art holy," "thou only art the Lord." When we too recognize the might of the Creator, the purity of the righteous God, the infinite mercy of the loving Father, then our only reaction can be to fall down and worship. The words "worship" and "worth" come from the same root. We worship because God is worthy.

Worship is our response to God's supreme worth

What followed with Isaiah in the Temple was also a part of worship. His response to the vision of God's holiness was a confession of his own unworthiness. There came also—and this is still part of worship—God's call to service. "Your sin is forgiven. . . . Who will go for us?" Isaiah's response was immediate: "Here I am! Send me." That response committed the prophet to a lifetime of service.

In the same way, Peter, on his knees in worship before

Jesus, heard him say, "Do not be afraid; henceforth you will be catching men." Peter's response was total commitment. He "left everything and followed him."

As to Isaiah, and to Peter, so to all worshipers come both a recognition of the supreme worth of God and a dedication of life to God. On God's side there is an acceptance of us as we are and forgiveness through Christ. Our response to the mercy of God comes in thanksgiving, praise, adoration, and service. We express these emotions through our prayers and songs and in the life we lead. "They left everything and followed him" describes worship as well as "he folded his hands" or "he knelt in prayer" or "he lifted up his voice in songs of praise."

Worship is both corporate and solitary

We think of Isaiah's experience as intensely personal, a time when the prophet stood alone before God. Yet it took place in the Temple and the language suggests that it was a time of ritual worship for the nation. Perhaps it happened at a great festival, when crowds thronged the Temple and Isaiah was taking part in the regular public worship.

Nor did Isaiah feel alone, for when he tried to communicate this overpowering experience to others, he spoke of heavenly creatures, the seraphim, joining in worship with him as they sang "Holy, holy, holy is the Lord of hosts. . . ."

In a sense any worshiper may experience the fellowship of other believers even though he is physically alone. Isaiah in the Temple or you in church are in a building associated with group worship, hallowed by its past, by the sacrifices of the people who built it and by the devotion of generations who have worshiped there. Certainly these influences strengthen our sense of God's presence. The ideas of our worship— what God is like, what pleases or grieves God—these, too, come from what you have been taught by others. Even when you read the Bible privately you read God's Word as it has come to you through hundreds of scribes and translators, prophets and priests and kings, Christ and Christians. Their personal witness is part of our own.

Our life of worship is both solitary and corporate whether we are alone or in a group. We may be in a large church, crowded with worshipers, taking part in an established ritual; yet even in this setting we are in one sense alone with God. The presence of other people fades away. We stand before him and all that matters is him and me. Or we may be alone in the privacy of our room, and as we turn our hearts to God, we are upheld by the communion of believers of all times and all places. A "cloud of witnesses" surrounds us. We share our common humanity. We share our common state as sons and heirs of God. We share our Christian fellowship. The most solitary worship is, in this sense, corporate, too. Indeed, corporate worship seems to be the normal form, and the times of solitary communion with God are extensions of that fundamental experience of worshiping God with others.

Nor do we fully understand what we are as Christians until we grasp our interdependence. We cannot exist religiously without Christ anymore than branches can live cut off from the vine. The solitary Christian is like an amputated hand if he does not sense that he, with his fellow worshipers, is the body of Christ.

This fellowship of worship is most alive to us when we recognize that we are upheld by other worshipers. At those times when our personal worship fails and grows flaccid, the corporate worship of the church sustains us. Our own spirits may flag, but we share in the aspirations of Christians of the whole communion of saints. We are sustained through the dry seasons of our spiritual life by the flow of living water in the lives of others.

Worship is based on our ideas of God

The kind of worship we have depends on what or whom we worship. When the Israelites came into Canaan they found there the worshipers of Molech, who threw their children into fire because they thought their god demanded this. Their kind of worship was determined by their idea of what their god was like.

Christian worship is determined by the Christian understanding of God. Our minds are involved as well as our emotions. As our study of the Bible and the instruction of the church help us learn more and more about God, our worship of him grows richer and more significant.

Christians worship a God who is approachable. "Lord, because it is thy will and command that we should come to thee and pray, we now come to satisfy thy desire," wrote Martin Luther.[3] When Jesus described for us what God is like, he pictured him as a waiting father, looking longingly for the approach of his prodigal son.

Because God is approachable, we respond by approaching him. Our search after God is a response to his search for us. We do not storm our way into his presence, but we accept his invitation and enter the door he opens.

Christians worship a God who is loving. We sum up his nature by saying that God is love. We have a larger understanding of him as love than as anything else. Because he is love, we respond in worship by returning love and sharing it. If God were not love, confession of sin would be a matter of dread. We come to a loving God, grieved and ashamed of our shortcomings, it is true, but confident that because he loves us he will forgive.

Christians worship a God who is holy, which means that our worship can never be cozy or a chummy relationship be-

[3] Clyde Manschreck, *Prayers of the Reformers* (Philadelphia: Muhlenberg Press, 1958), p. 1.

tween equals. God is holy and we are not. His ways are not our ways. Our response in worship of the holy God is an adoring recognition that here is one Person we cannot comprehend, a Goodness that casts into shadow our smallness and unholiness.

This holiness of God puts in us a response that we sometimes describe as fear. It is fear if we understand the fear of God to be an awe of his purity, a being overwhelmed by his greatness. It is never fear in the sense that we cringe before capricious temper or cruelty. In some primitive religions the worshiper lives in that kind of fear, fear of displeasing a malignant force or arousing the envy of a jealous spirit. Our Chistian fear rises from a sense of the immeasurable, incomprehensible glory and goodness of a God who loves us.

Christians worship a righteous God. His nature demands justice, honesty, goodness. His existence condemns all that is wrong or dishonest in our lives. We respond to this righteous God with a sharpened sense of injustice, with repentance for our wrongdoing, and with genuine effort to live a life constantly made better through his power.

Most of all, Christians worship God in Jesus Christ. Here is the God who puts aside his glory and becomes man so that he may win over estranged humanity. A God who gives of himself for us. Our response is loving worship and a life of loyal discipleship.

Worship involves all of our being

Since worship is a relationship between God and ourselves, there is no part of us that is not involved in it. Emotions are as important as understandings. And our patterns of action are equally significant. Sometimes we Lutherans tend to minimize our emotional responses. Yet awe, contrition, thankfulness, and love are all emotions. Unfeeling worship is not possible. We realize this when we have gone through

19

the forms of church worship without feeling the emotions they express. This lack of feeling is one of the dangers of the church service, or, indeed, of any kind of worship scheduled to be held at a certain time, whether or not we are prepared for it. At the same time, the use of the liturgy, associated with worship in other times and its proclamation of God's love and mercy, may rekindle the dying fires of devotion. If we always waited until we felt in the mood for worship, those times might be too infrequent.

Certainly, true worship involves our feelings, but an undue emphasis on emotions can lead to a self-centered worship based on the way *we* feel. Feeling must be disciplined.

Worship also involves our wills. We choose to approach God in worship, choose to make our spirits available to his grace. There are times when a real effort is necessary to keep our thoughts from straying, to take part in the liturgy when we are not in the mood or are weighed down by worry. This exercise of will, repeated and regular, can bring us increasingly to those times when our heart rushes to meet with God.

We believe that it is possible for children to have this living relationship with God which we call worship. As teachers of children it is our privilege to provide situations in which the child can become aware of this relationship. We can provide instruction so that he understands better the traditional worship pattern of the church and gains a more intelligent knowledge of his belief in God. We can encourage him to take part in the worship experiences of the group and also suggest that he can worship alone. More than this we cannot do, nor should we feel responsible to do more. With the child, as with every person, worship is a relationship which God initiates. We teachers sometimes are fellow worshipers. At other times we are bystanders—one of the cloud of witnesses.

How we know God loves u

Deborah Bahlinger—Primar

2

The Child at Worship

SALLY came into the family pew with her mother and father and two sisters. They sat down quietly and Sally closed her eyes to shut out all that was happening around her. "This is God's house," she said to herself. "He is here."

A fourth-grade class in Sunday church school had been studying the life of Jesus. When they read the story of his healing a little girl, Robin looked up, her eyes glowing. "Oh, don't you wish we could have been alive when Jesus lived?" she asked. The teacher recognized that this was the moment for worship. The group paused to pray.

When his father opened the big red book on the dining table, two-year-old Jeffy left his truck on the floor and climbed up on Daddy's lap. He knew that his family was going to talk to someone they loved, and Jeffy wanted to be part of the warm, loving circle.

Jack hoped he wouldn't be nervous when he came to read the passage from the Bible in the fifth-grade worship time. "Just think about the words you're reading," his teacher had said. So Jack read them again. "You have heard that it was said, 'You shall love your neighbor and hate your enemy.' But I say to you, Love your enemies and pray for those who persecute you, so that you may be sons of your Father who is in heaven; for he makes his sun rise on the evil and on the good, and sends rain on the just and on the unjust" (*Matthew 5:43-45*).

That wasn't easy to do, Jack thought to himself. And yet it was true that God sent rain to good people and to bad, so if you wanted to know God as your Father . . . Jack understood the verses as he read them.

These children all experienced worship, although the circumstances were different in each case. The church service was a formal occasion; the classroom and family, although informal, were planned times of worship. The Bible reading led to a spontaneous welling up of worship impulses, growing out of study. In each case the children knew that something was happening, something in which they were involved with God.

Child and adult are different in worship

Worship experiences are not the same for children and adults. It is true that for everyone, child or adult, the fundamental experience of worship is a relationship with God. But there are many ways in which this experience takes a different form with the child. That which means much to an adult may mean little to a child. There is, first of all, a basic difference between what a child and an adult can understand.

Much adult religious vocabulary is abstract. We speak of faith, eternity, grace, redemption. Even the ten-year-old is not yet ready to deal with many abstract terms or to generalize from his experiences. For the younger child ideas must be concrete and must deal with the specific things of here and now. A child younger than ten lives in the present; past or future mean little to him. How could he grasp the idea of eternity? So it is that some parts of the Bible which are most helpful in the worship life of the adult mean little to the child, and many of our fine hymns are sung by the child with a very limited understanding of what they really say.

Symbols play a large part in adult worship, but the child is quite literal in his understanding of terms. An adult may respond to the hymn "Rock of Ages" in a complicated way. He understands the literal picture summoned by the words; he realizes that a rock represents unchanging strength. He knows that the term is a poet's name for Jesus the Savior. More than that, the words evoke an emotional response compounded of recognition of his own helplessness, the welcome strength of Christ, the relationship of trust and dependence. But to young Gary a rock is a rock. Why the rock should be cleft, broken open, is more than he can know. That would seem to destroy its strength. As to what the rock has to do with Gary, or with Jesus, that is another of those mysterious ideas adults have. Since Gary is well behaved most of the time, he will sit through the singing of this hymn, perhaps even sing the words if he likes the tune, but nothing will happen to Gary. It is just another of those meaningless happenings in a world controlled by adults.

Some terms and symbols in religious thought are so important that they must be explained to the child, even though he finds them difficult to comprehend. We should make sure that we explain them in terms meaningful to the child. When we use material that has both a literal and a symbolic meaning, the child is likely to take the literal.

One morning parents were surprised to see their five-year-old son come into their room, plop down on the floor, and crawl under their bed. When he emerged a minute later his eyes were filled with tears. "I prayed last night for a dog and I thought God would leave it under the bed," he said.

"Why under *our* bed?" his father asked.

"Your window is wide open and mine is only open a little bit," said the child. "It would be easier for God to bring the dog in yours."

It took a great deal of patient explanation before the child understood that while God does hear our prayers, he does not answer them in that fashion. What seemed absurd to the adult seemed perfectly reasonable to the child, because his mind took a literal view of the way God answers prayer.

The child's frame of reference is limited compared to that of the adult. When the adult sings "A Mighty Fortress Is Our God," a thousand pictures and ideas form a background for the hymn. But the small child has not yet built up this background. He knows nothing of the Reformation or Luther's life, nor of the struggles in Europe when this hymn gave courage to people. We cannot count on these background values to give the hymn meaning. The child gets out of the hymn only what the hymn itself says.

Nor does the child bring to worship the same associations of past worship experiences that the adult brings. For the adult, the Sunday morning church service carries emotive values that result from times when that service has provided strength in time of trial or perplexity. The child, too, has some associations, but they are not the adult's. They may be briefer and fewer, but they are real. When he sits in the church pew with his parents, most likely he brings to his worship the feeling of belonging that comes from family life. He may bring a feeling of being uncomfortable, of being shushed up, of getting attention by little noises.

We must consider, too, that the child differs from the adult physically. One example of this is that most children simply cannot keep still as long as most adults. There are certain stages of growth when restlessness is almost constant. If our idea of participation in worship is keeping still, we will fail these children. We are asking them to do something they cannot do; by our insistence we are giving them the impression that worship and sitting still are synonymous.

The differences between child and adult should not be considered childhood deficiencies. The way the fifth-grader worships is right for that age. His behavior and understanding are part of a development process.

The worship of the child may have an immediacy and freshness about it that the adult is in danger of losing. The three-year-old who stood at the window and said, "God, are you going to make it rain all day?" lacked the maturity of an adult, but he had an intense consciousness of God which may fade from adult life. The sense of wonder about the world that adds so much to the child's response to the Creator too often gives place as he grows older to a view that sees nothing new or fresh in the world.

Another positive value lies in the fact that the small child has not yet acquired a religious vocabulary and therefore does not use words glibly. He is not so likely to say things he does not mean just because they sound pious. He has not, by over use, blunted the edge of the great words of religion. One concern about the older child is that he so rapidly learns the "right" answers, learns to say what you expect or want him to say rather than to express his own feelings.

Worship is a developing experience

While an adult can continue to grow in his worship life, with new insights from each day's experience, for the child this growing and developing is the outstanding characteristic. Simply getting older and growing bigger is no guarantee of growth in worship, but increasing experience and development of depth of thought help a child to more meaningful worship.

One of the children's magazines used to have a column contributed by the readers, "I used to think—." Blasé nine-year-olds would write from the heights of their maturity about the strange things they used to think were true when they were only six or seven. The Sixes and Sevens were just as amused at the ridiculous ideas they had when only four.

So pronounced is this growth in early years that although we may expect adults at worship to have a measure of similar attitudes and experiences, we cannot assume that a group of children whose ages vary even a few years will have understandings or responses that are common to all.

Compare the prayer life of a five-year-old and a twelve-year-old. When Jan was five, he told God about the flowers, about his new truck, about going downtown in the afternoon. Now that Jan is twelve, he sees that God speaks to him in many other ways; through the grandeur of natural beauty, through problems he thinks through, through the words of the Bible, the sermon on Sunday, the promptings of his conscience. He understands that prayer is much more than telling God things or asking for help. He has learned to include praise and adoration of the glory of God. He has learned to return thanksgiving for God's blessings. He realizes the need to confess his sins to God and ask for repentance, to pray for others as well as himself. He understands that prayer is a way of placing himself at God's disposal and allowing the Holy Spirit to work through him.

What a tremendous development this is in the space of seven years! It has been a steady growing, not a sudden leap from one extreme to the other.

At five, worship is a happy feeling that God loves us, a feeling expressed in spontaneous moments in the home or small groups, among people the child knows and trusts. Gradually the church building becomes a place where he learns about God and worships him in the company of other people. The liturgy of the church, which was something older people did, becomes a way he can express his own worship. When he is eleven, the child has a clearer understanding of the formal pattern of church life and of the symbolic way the church expresses her teachings. These matters, which had no meaning for him at five, have become significant vehicles of his worship.

We know that it would be unreasonable to expect the five-year-old to understand the meaning of the Trinity, or to find a certain passage in the Bible, or to pray in formal collects. Similarly, if we try to impose the worship behavior of an eight-year-old on a younger child, we will fail to have any meaningful results, and we risk giving him wrong ideas that he will need to unlearn later on. If at each age he can have experiences appropriate to his age, he will grow into a mature Christian in the fullest flowering of which he is capable. Each year's experiences will build on the foundation of the preceding years. The five-year-old was happy with stories about the baby of Christmas and Jesus the Friend who helped people. Using this as a foundation, each year should add to his understanding of Jesus as our Friend and Savior, until the older child will respond with loyalty to Jesus Christ as Lord.

Child and adult are alike in worship

Although there are very real differences in the understandings and feelings of the child and the adult, in many ways their worship experiences are alike. The fundamental insight, that worship is a relationship with God, is true of all worshipers, young or old. The child learns to know God as Creator, Father, Friend, Savior, Lord, and Guide. These are all relations, the Creator and the creature, the Father and child, the Friend and friend, the Savior and the one saved, the Lord and one who owes him allegiance, the Guide and the one who follows. The small child feels "I love you, God." The twelve-year-old is ready to say "I'll follow you, Lord Jesus." These are different ways of expressing the relation of love and discipleship, and the adult knows these, too.

In worship the child, as well as the adult, recognizes the supreme worth of God. His first understanding of God's greatness usually is derived from the world about him. God made the world, which is something not even parents can do.

The child thanks God for the flowers, the sunshine, the blue sky, all gifts that only God can give. He learns that he can trust in God's boundless love, even though the love of human beings has its limits. He senses the power of God, not only as the Maker of the world but as the one who knows all things, even our thoughts. This recognition has its most common expression in the way children thank God for a long list of things: for the world, for fathers and mothers, for food and home. It is present too in the underlying mood of love and trust that pervades significant worship.

The child, as well as the adult, responds to this recognition of God. "God made everything, every single thing," said the small child, expressing her sense of God's greatness. "Jesus is stronger than anybody," said the slightly older boy, admiration in his voice. Awe and wonder are not easily put into words, but these children expressed them in the terms of their ages. "We're just little," added another child, placing beside the greatness of God his own sense of humbleness. Adults often feel the same way.

In a Christian environment that child grows naturally from a sense of God's greatness to a sense of God's care. God made the world, which means that God made all that we need for life, food, warmth, shelter.

> God, who made the earth,
> The air, the sky, the sea,
> Who gave the light its birth,
> Careth for me.

The child responds to this perception with a rush of love, of thanksgiving. He sings this song with feeling because it mirrors his own understanding that the Creator cares for his creation. Compare this with the adult who sings "Praise to the Lord, the Almighty, the King of creation. . . ." The words are adult, but the response is the same.

The child is a little older when he begins to see that God is

30

good, morally good as well as good to us. Response in worship is primarily adoration, for we esteem what is good and adore that which is wholly good. This response is influenced by a sense of our own shortcomings, not always a sense of having done wrong, but the perception that at our best we are never radiantly good, as God is. To the child, wrongdoing is mainly just what the word implies, doing what is wrong, actions rather than attitudes. He recognizes the times he has been naughty, and is moved to tell God about them, sorrowfully because he has gained the understanding that such naughtiness grieves God. If the child's teaching has been truly Christian, this is sorrow at grieving someone he loves, not fear of an angry God. Although the child's sense of sin is more specific than the adult's both respond in the same fashion. Because God forgives and loves him the child responds with love which he expresses in words and songs, offerings and kindness to others. The adult does the same. As the child learns that God loves others as well, he reaches out to these others with love, trying to draw them into the circle of God's grace and love by sharing with them and praying for them. So do adults. Perhaps they respond with more reservations or caution, but the desire is the same.

The child, like the adult, worships in a context. He is surrounded and upheld by the influences contributed by others. He is helped by the building in which he worships, by the insights and example of older Christians. Like the adult, significant worship involves all of the child's being—his feelings and his understandings. What the child believes about God affects the way he worships. Even the youngest child bases his worship on what he believes. Three-year-old Teddy sings to himself "I love you, God," because he believes that God is nice and likes him.

Like the adult, the child has times of difficulty in worshiping. Ronnie and Hal got into a tussle outside the church. "I hate you," screamed Ronnie as Hal got the best of him. All during the church school session Ronnie glowered, stayed by himself. When worship time came he could not sing, he did not hear the words read from the Bible, and he sat stubbornly in his chair when the other children rose to pray. Our adult severence from worship is not often displayed so obviously, but none of us can easily experience the presence of God when we are feeling hatred or anger.

Preoccupations disturb worship for the child. If he is worried or frightened or simply too engrossed in some happening or idea, he may not be able to enter into the spirit of worship. Sometimes a transition is needed from a moment of other activity to a moment of worship. Quiet music helps with young children. A few moments of silence will give children time to quiet their muscles and minds.

Outside distractions interfere with an attitude of reverence. Loud noises in the hallway, visitors popping into the room, a pile of books falling over, anything like this can shatter the mood of worship. Children have not learned to ignore interruptions, so it is up to us to see that there are as few of these as possible. Sometimes a child cannot be in the mood for worship because he is physically uncomfortable. The chair is too big; his legs dangle. He cannot manage a hymnbook; he gives up trying to find the place. The surroundings of his room are dark; a sense of depression weighs on him. Mature saints have learned to disregard such impressions from the outside world, but children live in child bodies and cannot ignore their discomfort.

Nothing interferes with the mood of worship in small children so much as a feeling that the people around him are unfriendly or unkind. According to his temperament this feeling makes the child either curl up into a kind of armadillo or become a prickly porcupine, showing quills to all around. He needs a friendly atmosphere before he can show love.

Guiding children in worship

Although the worship life of children is something that we cannot manipulate or arrange—nor should we ever try to do this—the child does need our help and guidance. Our part is to provide opportunities for the child to worship and to do all that instruction and atmosphere can achieve to make his worship significant. Let us keep clear in our own minds what our purposes are as we involve ourselves in these worship experiences with the child.

1. *That the child may understand.* We can help the child to understand what is happening in worship. Worship is sub-standard if he only learns to repeat words that mean nothing to him.

Five-year-old Wendy likes to share her experiences. When she comes to visit, she "plays" the piano while she sings the church school songs she has just learned. One of the new songs was about "The V-I-V-L-E." Wendy did not know what it was, except that it was something you stand on. The other song had a catchy tune which was recognizable. But the words were "The pieces passes pieces passes—down in my heart—Tuesday!" How could singing this gibberish possibly mean anything in Wendy's worship life?

Worship materials we use should be suitable to the child's age. Even if Wendy had gotten the words right, the songs she was taught (?) were so adult in concept that she could not have understood their ideas.

Contrast Wendy's experiences with that of Polly. "What shall we sing today?" asked Mrs. Henry.

"Let's sing about 'God careth for me,'" said Polly promptly. "It makes me feel happy." This was Polly's favorite song. Each time she sang it she thought about God who made the earth and everything around her. The assurance that this wonderful God is also loving was reaffirmed every time she heard the words. Singing the hymn was a natural expression of her trust and love in God. It belonged in her worship.

Since our purpose is for the child to understand, we are led to provide instruction in worship. He must know a hymn before he can use it worshipfully. Some hymns require interpretation before they mean anything to a child. "A Mighty Fortress Is Our God" is a hymn that belongs in the usage of Protestant children, but it needs to be interpreted before a child can use it intelligently. Words like "fortress" need to be defined. Knowing the situation in which Luther wrote the hymn adds a great deal to its emotional impact. Awareness of its relation to Psalm 46 deepens its meaning.

In the same way instruction is needed so that children can worship through the liturgies of the church. Bible passages used in the liturgies gain new worship significance when they have been studied before hand.

2. *That the child may take part.* Worship is not your worship unless you are involved in it. The child may sit docile through well-planned worship services, but unless he takes part he is not worshiping. For the teacher this means an atmosphere of encouragement, so that the child will feel at home and relaxed in the group at worship. Older children may help to plan worship services in the church school and in this way feel more a part of the process. Understanding the worship service is a big step toward taking part in it. Familiarity helps greatly.

3. *That the child may relate each experience to his total life of worship.* The life of worship is a unity, with the relationship to God expressed at many times and places. Whatever we do in the church schools should fortify the child's personal devotions and strengthen his inclination to worship in the church with the congregation. (For this reason we are careful to avoid setting up worship in the church school that could rival or be a substitute for the church service.)

3

Unplanned Worship

HAVE you ever had a time when, walking through the woods on a beautiful October day, the beauty all about made you turn to the Creator in gratitude? This was not planned; suddenly you were aware of God. Or perhaps you had been thinking through a difficult problem and suddenly you saw what God wanted you to do. You were moved to ask for help.

Children have many of these moments of awareness, when they feel that God is very near. These moments could mean more if we who teach would be alert to them and be ready to divert our planned program to allow for them. Small children have their most significant moments of worship at times like these.

When Molly stopped in the doorway of the kindergarten room she noticed the flowers on the table. "Oh! Those flowers are pretty! Where did they come from?"

"I brought them," said her teacher.

"Where did you get them?"

"They grew in my garden," said the teacher.

"Who made them grow?"

"You know."

"God?" asked Molly.

"Yes, God."

"Because he loves us?" asked Molly, remembering. "Oh, thank you God, for making flowers grow!"

Paul preaching on a hill

Nancy Anderson
Grade 1

This kind of experience grows only in an atmosphere of love and trust. The small child often finds it in a home where parents are aware of God. He can find it in the church school too, if the atmosphere is reassuring. The room should be as attractive and cheerful as we can make it. There should be enough teachers and helpers so the child can have individual attention when he needs it. The teachers and helpers should be kind, gentle people who encourage love and trust in the child. Every effort should be made to avoid situations that frighten the new or timid child, such as overcrowding, loud or cross voices, a rigid plan that forces the child into disturbing conformity, an undisciplined class that provides no orderliness and security.

This spontaneous worship is important for all children, not just the preschool child. Adults should have it, too. Here are some occasions for this type of worship.

1. *Through informal conversation.* Times of talking together often provide opportunities for spontaneous worship. Patty came to her teacher at the beginning of the hour with tear-filled eyes. Her mother was sick; Patty was upset. The other children gathered around and were sympathetic. It was a natural transition to suggest that the group might want to ask God to help Patty's mother.

Some older boys and girls came to class with their minds full of a world crisis.

"There might be a war," said Dan, "and if they use atomic weapons . . . Boom! There goes the whole world."

"My dad says we'll go up to the lake next week *if* there is a next week," said Lynn.

"Miss Davis, aren't you worried? I am," said Janet.

"Yes, I'm worried," said Miss Davis, "but not sick."

"Why not?" asked Dan.

"Do you think that the people who are so scared are thinking at all about God?"

"I haven't heard anybody mention him," said Janet.

"Dan, get the Bibles and let's read Psalm 146," said Miss Davis. "I read it when the first bad news came and I think it has something to say to us."

"Put not your trust in princes. . . . Happy is he . . . whose hope is in the Lord his God, who made heaven and earth; . . . who keeps faith for ever. . . . The Lord watches over the sojourners. . . . The Lord will reign for ever."

"Let's read that psalm in our worship," said Dan. Miss Davis knew that they already had been worshiping.

"Mary Ann hasn't been here for three Sundays," said Mrs. Lennox. "Anybody know why?"

The third-graders looked uneasy. "Maybe we weren't very nice to her," said Susan in a small voice.

"Susan pushed her coat off the rack," said Dennis.

"Well, you grabbed her paper when we were going out," said Betty. "How do you suppose Mary Ann must feel?"

"I don't like her in our class," said Susan. "And her coat was dirty and I didn't want it next to mine."

"I wonder how Mary Ann feels," murmured Mrs. Lennox.

There was a long silence; then the children began to talk. Before they were through, they had reminded each other of many truths; that God loves all children, that he must be sorry that they treated Mary Ann like that, that it was wrong to be unkind. Finally Mrs. Lennox asked, "Do you think we should ask God to forgive us?" Heads were bowed and Mrs. Lennox put their feelings into words.

After they were finished Susan said, "If I'm really sorry, I'll tell Mary Ann so, won't I?"

"I will, too," said Dennis, "and we'll ask her to come back to our class."

Informal conversations lead to a genuine worship—thanks to alert teachers.

2. *As a result of study.* A study of the life of Christ, for example, may lead to moments of spontaneous worship.

Reading about Christian heroes can inspire boys and girls to thank God for such people and to ask God for help in becoming kind and brave. The wise teacher is alert to these opportunities. He will encourage his class to take the step from appreciation of these outstanding Christians, to thankfulness to God for such leaders and desire to follow their examples.

The Old Testament can lead children to understand that God controls the processes of history, that his will is related to the fortunes of countries in the world of today. The children are then but a step away from asking God to lead our nation to do right. Many times it depends on the teacher to make it possible for them to take that step.

The fifth-graders were studying Martin Rinkart's hymn "Now Thank We All Our God." They had memorized the first stanza. Now Jeanie was making a report on the background of the hymn. "It was a terrible time. Armies had tramped back and forth, fighting over that part of Germany, until every thing was just a wreck. I mean that. It really was a wreck. The whole country. Buildings had been destroyed and fields trampled down. It was a terrible time. And it went on and on and on."

"Seems like a queer time to write a hymn thanking God," said Craig.

"That's just it," said Jeanie. "It was a queer time if all you thank God for is good times and lots to eat. But you look at the hymn again. It doesn't say anything like that. Pastor Rinkart is thankful for God's love and that God never leaves us."

"I guess we have that," said Craig. "And a lot of things besides that Rinkart didn't have."

"We ought to thank God, too," said Marilyn.

Studying Bible passages can often merge into worship. These same fifth-graders had been working on the forty-sixth psalm as a choral reading. They had studied the meaning of each part of the psalm. They had memorized it and practiced it as a choral reading.

"Let's go over it again," said Miss Matthews. "This time as though we were in the church." The boys and girls straightened up, became quiet, and started to recite the psalm. Suddenly it was not just practice. The psalm had come to have meaning for them, and their recitation was an act of affirmation of their faith in God. They were worshiping.

3. *Outside the classroom.* Many of the happiest experiences of spontaneous worship come outside the classroom. Miss Andrews' class took a hike in the woods one Saturday morning. As they tramped along the path they came to a little knoll that overlooked a bend in the river. Emily, who was first, stopped. The others caught up with her. "It's like that verse," said Emily. "He has made everything beautiful in its time."

In another minute the group was shouting and playing, but for that moment they had lifted their hearts to God, the Maker of beauty. The verse that came to Emily's mind was one she had learned as a small child. Perhaps this was the most significant use she had ever made of it.

The four-year-olds were taken to visit the sanctuary of the church. The pastor explained to them that here was the place he stood to read the Bible, and here was the altar. The children sat on the front pew, legs stretched straight out in front of them—quiet now. None of them spoke for several minutes. The pastor continued to tell them about the chancel and sanctuary, where God and congregation worshiped. Their silence was a positive, active silence, when the presence of God was very real to them.

The teacher's role

"I don't know what you mean," said Mrs. Landis. "Unplanned moments of worship? I can't imagine my class in that kind of mood. It takes all my energy to keep them behaving and following my lesson plan."

The boys and girls in Mrs. Landis' class probably do not have moments of worship. They have fixed periods of worship or none at all. She has not surrounded them with the atmosphere of affection and trust in which such moments are apt to occur. Her relationship with her pupils is a kind of contest, to see if Mrs. Landis' plans will be carried out or if they can be upset by the youngsters. Mrs. Landis is intent on carrying out her plan, so she cannot be alert for opportunities she has not scheduled. What we are criticizing is certainly not that Mrs. Landis has a plan, but that her determination to carry it out leads to a disregard for the needs of her pupils and perhaps for the leadings of the Holy Spirit.

Mr. Ames *does* know how to go about having spontaneous worship—for it happens all the time in his class. The class atmosphere is filled with trust and affection. Mr. Ames comes to class prepared, not only with a plan, but with a spirit sensitive to the needs of his children and the opportunities for acknowledging the presence of God. His plans are flexible, ready to be put aside or changed to take advantage of these unplanned times for worship.

(From here on this book will be dealing chiefly with planned worship. The larger number of pages dealing with this more formal type of worship does not indicate that it is more important than the spontaneous moments. Both are vital. The unplanned worship is almost always sincere. Surely God is just as pleased with love that wells to the surface suddenly as he is with love expressed in careful preparation and deliberate form.)

How I know God loves me

Ellen
Anderson

4

Planned Worship

W HILE the spontaneous worship experiences of the child are important, they cannot supply all his needs. There mus be planned worship as well. Indeed, as we grow older and less spontaneous in all our approaches to life, these planned times become the pattern of our worship life. Planned worship helps us to keep our devotional life in balance, so that we do not depend too much on the impulses of the moment. For example, impulses might lead to an overemphasis on asking, on calling on God to help us, and too little time might be spent in dedicating our lives to serving him or simply giving thanks. Worshiping through the liturgies of the church helps keep various elements of worship in proportion.

When we consider the worship life of children we need to think both of their spontaneous moments and also of the planned worship of the church, of the church school, and of their family and private devotions.

The worship of the congregation

Look over your congregation at worship. Is it mostly made up of adults and young people? But there is three-year-old Barry sitting on his mother's lap, eight-year-old Linda with her family, ten-year-old Terry keeping an eye on his younger brother. What does this experience of worshiping God in the company of the congregation mean to any of these children? What goes on in the child's mind and heart?

The experience is not the same for every child, nor does

the child have the same experience every time he worships. From the actions and words of children we can deduce some of their reactions.

The child in church gains a sense of *community,* a sense of belonging to a big group. His baptism has made him a part of the group. He is there with people he knows and many whom he does not know. It is a group much larger than his family. God has called and gathered these people together. God has asked him to come and be with them, too. As the child grows older, he begins to get a sense of the past and his connection with it. He wonders about the people who built the church; he learns about people of long ago who also worshiped God. He can be helped to feel a sense of communion with these people and also with those distant men and women who wrote the hymns he sings, who wrote the Bible he hears, who used the liturgy he is using.

From the church at worship the child gains a sense of *security,* especially if he can lean against father's shoulder when The Service seems very long or share the hymnbook with his mother. As he becomes familiar with the building, with the hymnal, with the people who take part in the service, he feels secure. This is my church, this is my pastor. I am at home here.

Susan, whose family comes to church every Sunday, put her feeling of security in the church into charming words. She tilted her head to look up at the pastor at the door and said, "I'm going to call you Uncle Pastor." She felt secure with him and the community of the church just as she did with her family and relatives at home.

From the church the child gains a sense of *awe.* The bigness of the building is unlike the coziness of home. The focus on altar and candles and cross speaks of something different from everyday experiences. The "mystery" of the liturgy, with music and words that are like other music and words and yet different in tone, speaks of a Presence. The mystery is not the same as ignorance, for it is not destroyed as the child grows to understand it; the mystery deepens with growing experience.

There is also a sense of *joy*. There is something festive about a church service. People are in their best clothes and on their best behavior. There are flowers and lights and music. (Paul's favorite expression to describe Christians was that they were filled with joy.)

Is this too idyllic a picture of what happens to a child in church? Remember your own childhood; then look at children in church. Notice how little Barry sings—although he does not always sing the same tune as the others; notice how Linda sits relaxed and at ease, leaning against her mother; notice how Terry follows every part of The Service intently. Of course, children are not always absorbed in worship any more than adults are. We notice their lapses of interest because the child gives outward expression to his flagging attention with movements and noises.

If the child is to gain his highest experience of the church service, the church school must prepare him for it. We can encourage an attitude of love and respect for the church as the family of God. We can see that the child is acquainted with the people involved in the church service, such as the pastor, the organist, and the choir members. We can encourage an attitude of expectancy; something pleasant and good happens in the service of worship. Because our worship is based on what we believe, the teaching the child receives in the church schools about God, the Bible, and the church is important in his life of worship. Important, too, is the preparation that helps him understand the meaning of The Service and learn the prayers and hymns—all this to make his participation in church worship an intelligent, joyful, honest occasion.

Worship in the church school

Worshiping with the congregation helps the child understand that he belongs to the family of the church, which includes all ages. His church school class is limited to children of his own age. Church school worship is fragmentary, with particular facets of Christian knowledge or experience emphasized. The church service is a proclamation of the whole drama of redemption. Each time we take part in The Service we are reminded that God has created us, that we have separated ourselves from him by our sin, that he has sent Christ to redeem us, that we are upheld in fellowship with Christ in his church through the Holy Spirit.

The church school cannot present this full scope of Christian life, nor should it try to do so. *Church school worship is not a rival of The Service for the child's interest and attendance.*

Church schools are educational agencies, not designed for worship. So worship in the church schools is either the natural worship of groups of Christians studying together or worship that grows out of learning about worship and its forms. Church school worship gives the child the opportunity of worshiping with forms that he understands or is being taught to understand. He can ask questions on the spot. "I don't understand. What does it mean?" If the child thinks these questions during the church service, by the time he is free to ask them he has forgotten them.

The child can participate fully in the church schools because the atmosphere is less formal. Older children can help to plan whatever worship there is. Younger children can enter heartily into worship geared to their understanding. Little Barry sings in the church worship; his tunes are his own, without words. Certainly he is participating, but not in the full sense of the church school worship, where he knows the tunes and words.

In the church school the child worships with his own age group. His fellow worshipers may be his friends whom he will meet in school, at play, in other activities of their age. If the same people share both worship and the other parts of his life, worship and life are related for him. This may not be true in the large city church.

Worship in the church school gives the child an immediate chance to put into practice the knowledge or skills or attitudes he has learned in class as they relate to his relationship with God.

Family worship

In the intimate circle of the family the child can experience a closeness of fellowship in worship that he can gain in no other place. Here worship can be related, not only to his understanding and age level, but also to his day-by-day immediate concerns. It touches the most meaningful relations of the child's life.

In the new curriculum, classes for parents will give the concerned parent help in planning and conducting family worship. We who teach the children can help by encouraging the child to desire family worship and to take part in it eagerly.

Personal devotions

Every Christian needs times alone to worship God. The child needs these, too. From the practice of personal devotions the child gains the feeling that he can approach God by himself; no adult is needed to pave the way. When he is alone with God, the child can confide personal perplexities and problems that he would not tell to anyone else. He can listen to God without the distraction of other people. The worship proceeds at his own tempo, meets his own needs as it seldom can when directed by another person. In this personal communion with God the half-conscious aspirations and the dimly felt fears can be communicated with words.

The church school program can encourage the child to have his personal devotions. Discussion can present the idea to the child and suitable activity can help him put it into effect. Practice in making up prayers can help considerably.

Mrs. Rhodes' class talked about personal devotions and decided that the Advent season was a good time to begin. Under their teacher's guidance they made a worship booklet, with a Bible reference to read each day. After the date and the reference they left a wide space in which they planned to write some idea gained from reading the Bible verse. At Christmas two of the youngsters reported that not once had they missed their Advent devotions. Nearly everyone in the class had observed them a large part of the time. Given encouragement and a little guidance, these fourth-graders found the experience of personal devotions meaningful for them.

The third-graders made worship reminders for themselves. They selected pictures that would help them think about God (usually a picture of Jesus), and pasted the pictures on construction paper folded so that it would stand upright. Many of the third-graders put these reminders in their bedrooms and used them to focus their thoughts for personal prayers.

Class or department worship

When Janey went to St. John's church school in the old church building, her class of first-graders "assembled for worship." This meant that they marched from their class at a given signal and joined other boys and girls, Grades 1 through 6, for worship time. Then they sang hymns, had responsive reading, prayed, recited the creed, and made their offering. Now that St. John's has a new building, Janey's class of second-graders have worship right in their own class-room. The songs they sing are easier for Janey to understand because they have been chosen for her age. The words read from the Bible have something to do with the stories Janey hears. Nor does Miss Wilson have to stop in the middle of things to take them to worship. Janey likes it much better. It is better worship and better education.

Certainly having each class worship by itself is the ideal arrangement. Worship should be related to the day's study and held at the time it fits best into the day's routine. The child should find in worship an opportunity to respond to God's Word as he has met it during the other parts of the session. The materials used in worship should be studied and prepared so that they have their best use. All this is easier to do when a class worships by itself in its own room. Do not give up this ideal too easily. If it is not possible to have class worship in your present situation, think of it as a goal toward which you will work. Remember that a quiet prayer or the thoughtful reading of a hymn verse, or a portion of Scripture read reverently can lead to worship. These can be done in a crowded room.

Adaptations

Many of us have the job of doing the best we can to make our children's worship significant in situations less than ideal. At the very least, make every effort to have the preschool children in one separate group, children of elementary grades, (1 through 6) in a second group, and Grades 7 through 12 in a third group. It is much better if the three-year-olds are by themselves, the four- and five-year-olds in another group, and the school-age children divided as best you can. Grades 1 and 2 provide a natural unity since these children are not yet skilled enough in reading to be able to use printed materials and hymnals easily.

The following combinations are suggested, listed in the order of preference:

PLAN 1. Three-year-olds
Kindergarten, ages four and five
Grades 1 and 2
Grades 3 and 4
Grades 5 and 6
Grades 7 through 9
Grades 10 through 12
Young people through adult

PLAN 2. Three-year-olds
Kindergarten, ages four and five
Grades 1 and 2
Grades 3 through 6
Grades 7 through 12
Young people through adult

PLAN 3. Three-year-olds
Kindergarten, ages four and five
Grades 1 through 6
Grades 7 through 12
Young people through adult

PLAN 4. Preschool
Grades 1 through 6
Grades 7 through 12
Young people through adult

The setting for worship

There are no rules about the setting for worship except, obviously, that it should help the child worship. We try to avoid any distracting elements and make sure that everything we use helps his worship.

The room in which the children worship should be as attractive as it can be made. Sensory impressions are important to the child. Davey comprehends his world in terms of sounds, smells, feels, sights. When he comes into the classroom he is bombarded with impressions. If the room is cold, brown, if it smells like Mommy's mop, Davey will feel like holding back, drawing inside himself to avoid the unpleasant impressions. His teacher's efforts to create an atmosphere for worship are handicapped.

"What a difference in the children since we painted this room," said a teacher. The walls had been changed from the ugly liverish brown to a soft, restful shade of green. The children were quieter, more co-operative, and happier with the new color.

Sometimes the necessary change is achieved by a greater degree of orderliness. Dirty windows, paper-littered floor, furniture askew, materials stacked in a corner instead of stored away—what a picture! How can children respond with a spirit of reverence to this atmosphere of "nobody cares"?

The setting for worship in the church school may be varied. At times you may be able to take your class into the nave of the church for their worship. Sometimes you may take the children out doors and worship there.

The third-graders were learning about the Feast of Booths, when the ancient Israelites gave thanksgiving by worshiping in outdoor shelters. Energetic Miss Barto persuaded Mike's daddy to build one on the church lawn. The children brought fruit as their offering, planned to take it as a gift to someone after their service. As they worshiped on the lawn, the distant Hebrew festival came to life. The children knew how those long ago people felt, thanking God for the fruits of the field. More important, as they worshiped in this new setting they felt thankful for the food which they usually took for granted.

If your group is small you have more freedom to try new ways. Sometimes you may worship very simply, with your group in a circle of chairs. At other times you may wish to have a focus for your worship, a table or shelf on which flowers or an open Bible help to center the attention of the children. In the Advent season lighting the candles of the Advent wreath may be made a helpful experience. Whatever you do, the children should understand the reason for it, so that the arrangements will be a help and not a puzzling distraction.

There is a difference of opinion as to the place of replica altars in the church school rooms. Those who favor their use believe the altar provides a natural center for worship and gives the children instruction in worshiping with the altar in the church. Those who do not favor the use of an altar feel it sets up a kind of service that rivals or supplants the church service itself.

Luther D. Reed says; "The altar is the table of the Lord and the place of benediction. These are its sacramental connections. It is also the place where vows of fidelity and consecration are spoken and where the united prayer of the congregation is offered. These are its sacrificial or subjective features."[4]

This definition does not sound appropriate for a church school altar. Can an altar, therefore, be used rightly anywhere other than in the sanctuary of the church? (Perhaps in emergencies, as in field services with the armed forces, but the congregation's children have the church altar available. The church school is not an emergency situation.)

Most important, the setting for worship should be as free from distraction as you can make it. It should be as quiet as you can manage. Discourage errands that bring people in and out of your room. Close the door on the noise in the hallway or out on the street. This quiet is especially important for prayer.

Elaborate settings or services prove distracting to most

[4] Luther D. Reed, *Worship* (Philadelphia: Muhlenberg Press, 1959), p. 24.

Linda Dewees—Grade 5

children. Too many things to look at, too many pages to find, too many things to remember, too much moving around— simple worship is best.

Sometimes we overlook the distracting influence of being uncomfortable. If Johnny is sitting in a chair that is too big, so that his legs dangle in space, it takes heroic effort to keep his mind on his worship. If the room is too hot, or the air stuffy, or the sun shining right into the child's eyes, these explain why he is so restless and so removed from the spirit of worship. As he grows older we hope he will learn to cope with discomfort and distraction, but for the time being it is our responsibility to avoid it for him.

The time for worship

The time at which we worship need not always be the same. It is possible that in some session plans worship might come in the middle of the period, or that a plan might be changed to allow the time for worship to come when the class is ready for it!

The great disadvantage of always having worship at the beginning of the session is that too often this clearly marks it as "opening exercises." It then becomes something to take up time until everyone has arrived. If you prefer to have your worship first, or have no choice about it, guard the time so that it will be truly worship. Be on hand early so that preliminary work can be carried on and the children ready for worship. If you are always early, your children are more likely to come on time and you will avoid the interruptions of one arrival after another.

There are advantages in having worship at the end of the session. You can help your children be ready for it. If they are to take part, all the arrangements can be made. Worship can come as a climax to the study, enriching both study and worship. If the class has been studying a hymn, it is logical to use that hymn in worship after the study. When its use is postponed until the beginning of the next session, there will be some loss in continuity of thought. If a class project is to memorize a passage of Scripture, there is an added incentive to the memorization if it will be used in the day's worship. If a class has been studying the way the prophet Jeremiah brought the Word of God to men, effective use of passages from the Book of Jeremiah will add to the impact of the worship and give added insight to the recollection of the study.

The amount of time needed for worship will vary with the age group, the season of the year, and the lesson theme. No rules can be given. In a class session of one hour and fifteen minutes, ten to fifteen minutes of worship is usually enough for children in Grade 7 and above to spend on worship and worship instruction combined. Younger children may need more time if instruction in worship and music is included. Of course, preschool children will have most of their worship times come throughout the session, whenever it fits into the development. Many of these times will be spontaneous and all of them will be brief. The teacher's guides for your courses will provide helps for planning worship to fit the situation.

We think of worship in the classroom as being only one of the worship experiences of the child. We expect him to have times of worship in the church with the rest of the congregation and regular periods of devotion in the circle of his family and by himself. And yet worship in the classroom may be the only occasion in which we can be sure he is involved. All the more reason for making it as helpful as possible.

The elements of worship

It was the first time that Jerry and Nancy had ever planned worship for the class.

"How do we go about this, anyway?" asked Jerry.

"Think about the worship we usually have," said Nancy. "What goes in it? We sing, don't we? And pray."

"There's the offering," said Jerry, "and we read from the Bible. That seems to be about what we do. I wonder why we always do it that way."

Too often we do it that way because we are following a pattern, without questioning the reasons for it. Jerry and Nancy have described the basic elements in a worship program, but what are the reasons for these elements?

We go back to our fundamental description of worship as a relationship with God. Something must happen between God and the child who worships. We realize that it is God who initiates the relationship. It is God who reaches out to the child long before the child is aware of him. He speaks primarily in his Word, through the Bible. Therefore, one important element in worship is hearing God's Word.

In our planned worship in the church school, the child hears God's Word as we read the Bible. As he listens he learns what God offers to him in the way of a loving relation through Jesus, and he also hears what God requires. Congregational worship has always given a large place to the Word of God as we hear it read in the lessons and taught in the sermon. In church school worship the Bible will have an important role, just as the church school study places much emphasis on understanding the Bible better.

Our use of the Bible in worship must be related to our understanding of it through study. The child is not really hearing God's Word if it is meaningless to him. He must understand so that the Word can enter into his mind and life. Using the Bible in worship adds a new depth to his study.

Worship has a back-and-forth movement in which the worshiper is at times receptive, at times active. A second element in our worship is expressing our praise and adoration. In church school worship this usually takes the form of song and prayer. Music helps the child express his joys. Praise that would be spoken in hushed, unaccustomed words can be sung joyously, without restraint. Adoration that sounds stifled and inept bursts forth in satisfying words and tones as he sings hymns of praise.

The Psalms, which were originally the hymns of the Jewish people, are another way of expressing praise.

Praise the Lord!
Praise the Lord, O my soul!
I will praise the Lord as long as I live;
I will sing praises to my God while I have being (Psalm 146:1, 2).

Another element in the child's worship is conversation with God, the prayers he offers and the silences in which he listens. The child can learn to know many ways of talking with God; silent prayer, spoken prayer, prayers that have been written. As he grows older he will find help in using the prayers of the church, the collects that have been the vehicle of prayer for so many people over so many years.

If the child is to have a satisfying life of worship, we must help him learn the many kinds of prayer. Too many of us never outgrow an idea of prayer as asking God for gifts. What an impoverished relation with a loving father! In our planning let us make sure that prayers lead the child into the wide reaches of communication with God. Prayers should express the adoration and praise that any clear-sighted thought of God will inspire. The overwhelming aspect of God is not what he gives, but what he *is*. We praise and adore him for his majesty and glory, his righteousness and loving-kindness. We thank him for his mercy. We confess our own shortcomings and ask him for forgiveness. We ask him for his help and we intercede for others. These are rightful kinds of prayer and there are others. Let us help the child to enjoy all the riches of prayer.

Offering God our gifts and our lives is another element of our worship. When we love someone, we want to give them some expression of our love. The little child stops his play to pick a flower and bring it in to mommy or daddy. He gives because he loves. When he loves God he has the same desire to give. So do we. We need to remember that even the offering is a means of responding to God's grace. The offering can be an important part of our worship. We should feel thwarted when, in worship, we have no opportunity to make some kind of offering. Yet it certainly need not always be money! In fact, in congregations with a unified budget, no offering of money may be made in the church schools. But in many churches, the offering still is part of the worship.

"Why can't I have envelopes for the building fund?" asked Dennis. "It's my church, too, isn't it?"

Dennis came from a family where giving to the church was a joyful sharing that had a place in the family budget. He had heard plans for the new church building discussed eagerly. This was an important adventure and he wanted to have a part. His parents talked with him, helped him plan to manage his spending money so that he would have something to give to the church. Placing his envelope in the offering of the church became a real part of his worship.

We cannot depend on all children having family training in stewardship such as Dennis had. Too many of them come prepared to give only small change that doesn't cost them anything. If our teaching and our example encourage the child to give only what does not matter, the offering will not be a significant part of worship. But if the child catches a glimpse of what Christian stewardship really is, a free giving of time and ability, the act of making his offering of money or talent or time can be a deep worship experience.

The child should feel a connection between offering his gifts and dedicating his life. In the church service the offering of our gifts is followed by the Offertory, which expresses the offering of our lives: "Create in me a clean heart, O God."

Not only should the child see the offering as his response to God's love by giving, but it is also a way of expressing our love for God by helping God's other children. What the church can do for people because we have offered our money and time is an exciting story. Finding out about the work of the church will give new meaning to our worship in the offering. So too will projects in which children make things for other people or visit shut-ins. So too will making a scrapbook for a hospital ward or singing Christmas carols for older folks or taking an Easter lily to someone who is sick.

Planning for worship

The first step in planning worship should be a consideration of the objectives of the course and an understanding of
the way the worship will fit in with these goals. Worship
should be related to the study, and grow out of it. Suggestions for worship included in the teacher's guide should be
weighed and any necessary adaptations to the local situation
made.

Projects and activities for the term should be studied in
their relation to worship. Miss Christopher's class is drawing
a mural that could be used as a focus for worship. Will Miss
O'Neill's boys and girls be writing a litany that could be
helpful? Can the choral reading from Mrs. Friend's class be
a way of presenting God's Word?

If worship results in a desire to share something with
others outside the church school, will the teachers be ready
to guide?

If the church school worship goes beyond individual
classes, time should be scheduled for instruction in worship.
"All Creatures of Our God and King" is a hymn that will be
used in the worship but not all the children know it. When
will the hymn be taught to the children? Who will do it?
Miss Bailey's class is planning to attend church as a class one
Sunday. Instruction in the meaning of The Service will make
this experience more valuable. When should the instruction
take place? Where?

In many schools, space and materials must be shared.
Supervisors should plan ahead so that teachers will have the
rooms they need, that Bibles, hymnals, and pianos will be
available.

Important in the planning will be the goal to have each
child participate in worship. Is Jerry a problem? Mrs. Friend
taught Jerry last year and understands him. She suggests
that he needs to be given definite responsibilities. Ask him

to see that the hymnals are on hand. If he has a part to play, he will not try to disrupt the worship.

Children can plan

Once this general planning is done, children of school age can help to plan session worship. In first and second grades their part may be only to say a verse that the teacher asks them to say, but even this needs planning. Boys and girls should understand that it is an important task to bring Bible messages to others and we practice saying or reading the verses clearly so that the others can hear and understand. Third-graders are able to read short parts of the Bible for class worship.

Beginning with fourth-graders, children are able to meet in small committees and plan what material shall be used in worship as well as who shall take part. As they grow older the children need less and less overt guidance from the teacher. If, from their earliest planning with the teacher, the children are taught to consider why materials are chosen for worship and learn that worship grows out of study, their planning can be very good indeed. Their planning can educate them in the meaning of worship, as they weigh the reasons for using one hymn rather than another and advance from choosing a hymn with a catchy rhythm to choosing the hymn that best expresses the ideas being studied.

The more the children help in the planning, the more the worship will be their own and their participation genuine and enthusiastic. But the teacher should guide sufficiently so that the lesson plans and objectives are strengthened and not ignored.

5

Instruction in Worship

"I HAVE come over to play with Mary," said Gertrude, leading her small brother by the hand. Since this was Gertrude's first year in school, the living room quickly became a school room, with Gertrude as teacher and the younger children her pupils. Gertrude attended a Roman Catholic school so she needed a scarf for her head so she could pretend to be "Sister," and teach her pupils a prayer.

One phrase was repeated again and again. Mary's mother stood in the doorway to listen. "Partly do we repent our sins," said the pupils after their little teacher. The mother smiled as she recalled the original phrase Gertrude was supposed to have learned—"Heartily do we repent." Perhaps "partly" was a more accurate prayer, she thought to herself.

Children learn what they think they hear, not what we think they hear or what we mean them to hear. Gertrude heard "partly" and learned the prayer in that form.

Instruction in worship

Our ideal of worship is a free-flowing relationship between the child and God, and yet to achieve that ideal, instruction in the ways of worship is needed. We achieve our objective of worship experiences that are meaningful to the child only when he understands, takes part, and relates worship to his life.

1. *To help him understand.* Gertrude learned a prayer

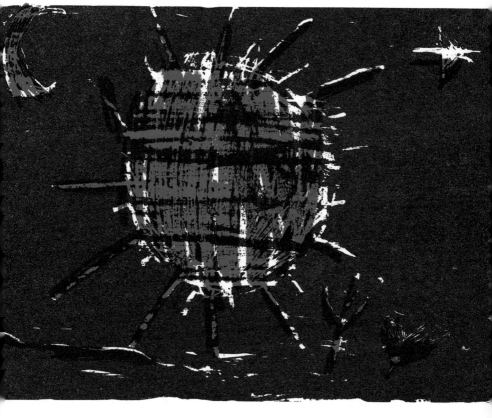

King of creation   Lynne Douglass—Grade 1

whose meaning was changed because she used the wrong word. We want our children to understand correctly the words they use in worship. A story (which may be apocryphal) is told of Theodore Roosevelt, who as a small child became afraid of going to church. He had heard a Bible verse that frightened him: "For the zeal of thine house hath eaten me up" *(Psalm 69:9 King James Version)*. What could a zeal be? Obviously something that could eat you up, like a lion or a bear. The imaginative child pictured a mysterious animal lurking in the church, ready to pounce on him.

Children's religious experience is likely to be full of these misunderstandings. Because the words are familiar to us adults, we forget that the vocabulary of worship contains many words and phrases that either mean nothing at all to the child or mean something quite different from their correct meaning. How many of these words would be understood by the children you teach? (Confess, beseech, grant, transgressions, Redeemer, refuge, infinite, implore, remission, Holy Ghost) They are all used in the first ten minutes of The Service of our church. Perhaps children may grasp something of the meaning from the general tenor of the prayers, but more likely they do not.

Nor is it only the words we use in worship that are not understood. Many of our ideas are puzzling or misleading to the child if they are not explained.

We need to give instruction so that the child may understand the actions of our worship. Why must we keep quiet in church? Why do we bow our heads in prayer? Why do we stand at certain times in the service? Why do we place offerings on the altar? Why do we kneel? There is a reason for everything we do and if the child understands the reason he will find his worship more significant.

2. *To help him take part.* Three-year-old Gary comes to the early service with his family. When the congregation

sings Gary sings; not the words or even the tune, but he sings. Occasionally he keeps on singing after the others have stopped. You might say he is participating, but we hope that when Gary is older he will take part in the congregation's worship by singing the same words and melody as the rest of us, and that he will understand what he is singing. Gary will need some instruction before he is ready to do this.

Watch children in the church school when a hymn they do not know is planned as part of their worship. They do not sing, or do so half-heartedly, with minds wandering from the worship as surely as their eyes stray from the hymnal. Worship is not the time to learn a hymn; the learning should take place before the worship begins.

"Bless—bless—blessed are you when men—I don't know the next word—" read Mary.

"Revile," said Miss Burgess.

"Revile you and—"

"Persecute," said Miss Burgess.

"Pursecute you and—"

"Utter," said Miss Burgess.

"Utter vile you—oh, oh, I've got the wrong line—"

Larry punched Bobby. Marlene giggled. "Children, you aren't paying attention," said Miss Burgess. "This is worship, you know."

Was it? How much worshiping was any child doing? Poor Mary, struggling with words she did not know, certainly did not hear the Word of God in the Bible verses she was trying to read. Her reading certainly did not proclaim the gospel to Larry and Bobby and Marlene since they could not make any sense of what they heard.

Before this selection from the Beatitudes could be used meaningfully in worship, the children should have become acquainted with its meaning. Before Mary read anything from the Bible for worship, she should have practiced it so that she could read intelligibly. This could have been a real experience of hearing God's Word in worship if Mary had read, with skill and understanding, a part of the Bible that the group had studied.

Even small children need instruction in worship. They need to know that we can talk to God, that he will listen because he loves us. They need to learn that when we pray we are talking to God, that when we sing, we sing about him and to him. Someone must see to it that they are singing words that have meaning and not gibberish, that they know why they sing.

3. *To help him relate worship to his life.* Children do not see automatically the relation of what they do in church school to the worship of the church or the home or their personal devotions. If we help them to understand that worship is not limited to the classroom but that the present experience is related to other times of worship, they will have made a big step toward understanding that worship pervades all of life.

Sometimes we are startled when we observe Ellen, who has seemed so devout in class worship, outside the church slapping her little sister. Evidently Ellen has not seen any relation between her worship and her daily attitudes. She needs instruction at this point. She needs to learn that the worship of our lives is related to the worship of our lips.

Learning the liturgy

At the fifth-grade level of the Sunday school, children spend a whole term studying worship, with a great deal of time and attention spent on the liturgy of the church. Is it really that important to children?

Imagine the survivors of a hypothetical shipwreck stranded on the usual hypothetical desert island, with nothing in the way of religious education except their knowledge of the liturgy of the church. Would there be any chance of Christianity surviving among them? Indeed, yes, for in the liturgy of the church they would possess the essentials of Christian belief. The Service is not merely an artistic arrangement of fine sounding words and music; it is a statement of our Christian faith.

Think of what we believe. We believe in God, who created the world and man. We believe that man by his own sin has estranged himself from God; he cannot live in this estrangement and yet he is unable to overcome the barrier. But God, in his great love, has reached out to man, offering him forgiveness and oneness with him. For this reason he has sent Jesus Christ to win us back to God. Through him we can be restored to our intended relation to God as his loving children. His Holy Spirit continues to guide us as we find our Christian fellowship in the church.

In The Service these basic themes are expressed and amplified. The introduction to The Service, the Confession of Sins, directs our thoughts to the Lord who made heaven and earth. It expresses our sinfulness and helps us to flee for refuge to the infinite mercy of God, asking his forgiveness for the sake of the Lord Jesus Christ. Here is the heart of Christian belief.

Not only confession, but all the forms of worship are expressed in The Service. We give voice to our praise and adoration as we sing the *Gloria* and the *Gloria in Excelsis*. The Collect and the Prayer of the Church express our petition and intercession. The *Kyrie* embraces the whole world in our intercession. We listen to God's Word, not only in the lessons for the day, but also in the sermon and in the declaration of forgiveness that follows our confession. And we are given opportunities to respond to God's grace with a resolution to witness and to share as we stand to recite the Creed and as we make our offerings of God's kingdom. We commune in a special way with God and our fellow Christians in the Sacrament.

To most people the only "church" they know is The Service. It is important that children be instructed so they will know and understand it, take part in it, and relate it to their lives.

Two third-graders asked their church school teacher if they could go to church with her. It was a Communion service, the first these children had ever seen. They were excited as people went up to the altar. "What are they doing?" they demanded in whispers. "Why?"

If the teacher had been foresighted enough to talk with the children about the Communion, to explain what happened and the reason for its observance, this would have been a most impressive experience. As it was, they were more puzzled than impressed.

We do not wait until our children are in the fifth-grade course before helping them to understand something of worship in the church service. Our aim is not to make liturgical experts of them or to offer them facts about The Service but to help them grow to love the experience of worshiping with the congregation.

Children learn something from a visit to the church sanctuary. People come to this impressive place to worship God. They sing songs to praise God. They tell him they are sorry for being wrong. They learn more about what God wants of them. The people who come to church are like a big family. The family includes children.

One teacher who took her small children on such a visit followed it by stopping at the church office. The parish worker opened the file where the cards of church membership were kept and hunted up the card for each of the children. As the child looked at the card with his own name on it, he realized that he belonged to this church family. This experience strengthened his feelings about worship.

Another teacher, with slightly older children, helped them to find Collect 17, page 221, "For the Children of the Church," as a way of realizing that they belonged to the church.

Attending The Service is a way of getting deeper understanding of what the church really is. Parents often ask for advice. Should they bring Chuckie to church? How does one make him behave? Suppose he is restless?

There are no clear-cut rules. Children are different, as any mother of more than one child knows. Tony is always good in church ("good" here means quiet). His brother Jimmy simply cannot sit still. Tony could go with his parents when he was three. Jimmy cannot attend until he has learned to sit still in school. There is no rule, except that going to church should be a happy experience for both the child and the rest of the congregation. We can explain to the child that out of consideration for other people it is necessary to be quiet during The Service, that we can help other people worship by our quietness; but the church service should never be a battleground between active child and determined parent. After a child goes to school he is physically able to sit through one hour of church. Whether or not he is willing to do so depends a great deal on the family atmosphere. If parents attend church because they love to do so, small children often catch this spirit.

It is a pleasure to see a family like the Powells, who bring their children to church. The two older children now take part in The Service; four-year-old Connie just relaxes in the pew, her head against her father's side. She shares in something her family is doing.

The worship plans for the church school group should always grow out of the lesson material and be related to the unit objectives, but there are times when a relation to a liturgy can be pointed out incidentally. The teacher may comment, "We use these words in the church service, too." If Bible passages used in study are the same as the lessons read in church, or as parts of a liturgy, this could be noted. When we read of the song of the angels to the shepherds in the Christmas story, you might say, "Every Sunday in church we sing the angels' song 'Glory to God in the highest, and on earth peace, good will toward men.'"

Miss Siddons found her fourth-graders, who sang in the junior choir, so interested in the terms used in worship that they made a glossary and kept it in their classroom. The teacher made no effort to teach the meaning of these words, but the list of words and definitions was there for everyone to consult if they wanted to. Their glossary began like this:

ALLELUIA: A Hebrew word meaning "Praise ye the Lord."

AMEN: Hebrew for "So be it."

COLLECT: A prayer.

CREED: What we believe.

EPISTLE: A letter in the New Testament.

GLORIA IN EXCELSIS: Latin for "Glory in the highest."

GLORIA PATRI: Latin for "Glory to the Father."

INTROIT: Latin for "He enters." The Introit is made up of verses from Psalms.

KYRIE: Greek for "Lord."

OFFERTORY: A chant sung at the time of the offering. Its words are taken from the Psalms.

When people speak of learning the liturgy, they most often mean learning to sing the musical setting. This instruction in music will likely be the work of the junior choirs or the director of music. Even if you are not a music teacher, you may help your boys and girls to appreciate the music of the church's services. Recordings of The Service are available and your group might listen to them. And don't forget *Matins* and *Vespers*.

Much instruction in worship will be an incidental part of

the class study, but occasionally it will be profitable to schedule time for learning hymns or the musical setting of The Service.

The child will get more out of The Service if we explain a few points of good church manners. Other people are there to worship, just as he is. We do all we can to help others worship. We take part as much as we can and keep from doing anything annoying, such as whispering or moving about. Behavior in church should be presented in this positive manner, as Christian helpfulness for others, rather than negatively with "It's wrong to be noisy in church. . . . Don't . . . Don't!"

Teaching children to pray

Prayer is a natural turning to God, a conversation. The child needs to learn this. Is it not a natural thing that he picks up from his environment?

Undoubtedly some children turn to God in prayer almost instinctively, because they are growing up in an atmosphere where people are aware of God's presence. That is not true of all children. Many people live as if there were no God. We cannot truly rely on the child's environment to teach him to pray. It is the church which must provide an atmosphere in which prayer seems natural and in which conversations with God can flourish.

This is deeper than teaching children to say prayers. A group of teachers were exchanging experiences about vacation church school. One teacher said she had been very successful in getting her fourth-graders to take part in a prayer circle every morning. "Oh there were a couple of boys who didn't want to pray," she said, "but I told them they couldn't make things in our activity period if they didn't pray, and after that they prayed as nice as could be!"

Where could we find a better example of what not to do?

This teacher not only failed to teach her children what prayer is, but she taught them that it is something which it is not.

Even our sincere prayers sometimes have so limited a range that we have scarcely glimpsed the mainland of prayer. If our prayers are mainly petitions, or if we resort to prayer only in times of stress or danger, we have not begun to enjoy the richness of this conversation with God. Children need help in exploring the reaches of prayer beyond the self-centered asking.

How can we teach children to pray? First of all by talking with them about it, so that they come to know what we mean when we say "prayer." Reassure the child that he can pray, that God is a loving Father, eager to hear and to talk with him. The child needs to know that God does not use words the way we do. He answers by giving us ideas or by changing things in our lives.

With small children the teacher's example is the best way to teach about prayer. When Susan brought a bouquet of flowers to the church school, all the children enjoyed them. Miss Andrews said, "I feel like saying thank you to God for his lovely flowers." So she bowed her head and said, simply, "Thank you, God, for the beautiful flowers." The children followed her example; they bowed their heads and felt her words as their prayer, too. If there are times when food is served to the children, the teacher may say, "We want to thank God for our food." As she says a simple grace the children are learning that Christians thank God for his gift of food, and learning how to do it.

Christians of all ages can enter into silent prayer as a leader guides their thoughts.

"Shall we pray for Marcia, who is in the hospital?" asked Mrs. Carody. "We'll ask God to take care of her and to bless the doctors and nurses who help." Heads bowed, the children prayed in their own thoughts. The group felt a oneness in prayer although each child thought his own silent petition.

These same methods may be used with older children if they are adapted to their age. But the range of ways to teach about prayer grows larger as the child grows older. The Bible has many stories of people who prayed, stories which can be used with children of school age. Jesus told a story of two men who went to the Temple to pray (*Luke 18:10-14*). The one man "prayed with himself." He wanted God to hear what a fine man he was, how well he observed the Law. He called God's attention to the unsatisfactory conduct of other men, which made his own life shine all the brighter. The second man came to God confessing that he was not good and asking God's forgiveness. Children can understand that the first man was not praying and that the second man was.

Another illuminating story about prayer is found in Genesis 32:3-12. After a long absence Jacob was returning home to meet his brother Esau. Because Jacob had cheated Esau years earlier he had reason to be afraid of him. When the messengers he sent ahead came back to Jacob with the news that Esau was coming to meet him, accompanied by four hundred men, Jacob was afraid. He divided his company into two parts, thinking that if Esau destroyed one of the parts, the other might escape. Then Jacob prayed to God, "I am not worthy of the least of all the steadfast love and all the faithfulness which thou has shown. . . . Deliver me, I pray thee, from the hand of my brother, . . . for I fear him. . . ." Across all the centuries that moment of fear comes to us in a vivid picture. Here is a man afraid for his life and the lives of his family. He calls on God for help; but his approach to God is an honest one, for God has blessed him more than he ever deserved. His experience of God's steadfast love makes him dare to ask even more of God, that he will save him from the present danger.

Still another kind of prayer is demonstrated in the story of

Daniel (*Daniel 6*). Darius, the Persian king, had singled out Daniel, the Jew, by giving him a high office in the kingdom. Jealous men persuaded the king to sign a foolish decree that anyone who made a petition to any god or man for thirty days, except to King Darius, should be cast into a den of lions. This law was designed to trap Daniel, for they knew that he worshiped God every day. When Daniel knew that the law was signed, he went to his room, knelt and "prayed and gave thanks before his God, as he had done previously." Daniel's faithfulness to God even when in danger is an example children can admire. (The lion's den is not important at this point.)

Hearing about these people who prayed, the child sees that there are many kinds of prayers. The man in Jesus' story confessed his sin and asked for forgiveness. Daniel gave thanks—and this was before his rescue from the lions. Isaiah replied to God, "Here I am! Send me." Jesus prayed, "Thy will be done."

Here are some familiar prayer examples:

PRAISE AND ADORATION
Psalm 117, and many others
Revelation 4:8—"Holy, holy, holy, is the Lord God Almighty, who was and is and is to come!"
The Gloria Patri
Hymn 76 in the new children's hymnal—"All Creatures of Our God and King"
Confession—The first part of The Service, *Psalm 130, 1 Chronicles 21:8*

THANKSGIVING
Psalm 136, and many others
1 Chronicles 29:10-13—David's prayer when the nation crowned his son Solomon as king

INTERCESSION
Exodus 32:31—Moses prayed for his people
Acts 12:5—The church was praying for Peter
The Kyrie—in The Service, we pray for others

2 Chronicles 1:8-10—Solomon prayed for wisdom
Genesis 32:9-12—In time of danger Jacob prayed for deliverance from his brother Esau

In the Prayer of the Church, in The Service, many types of prayer are gathered together. We give thee praise and many thanks. . . . we intercede for the church Universal, for our rulers, for our homes, for those in sorrow or need. We ask God to give us peace, his blessing on seed time and harvest, . . . and bring us at length to the joy of the heavenly kingdom.

It is comparatively easy to lead the child to genuine expressions of praise and thanksgiving, but we are not so successful with prayers of penitence. The reason is that too often we expect the child to be penitent because he has caused us an inconvenience.

Janet was early for church school. She decided to be helpful and surprise Mrs. Face by having all the supplies on the table. She got down the big jar of paste and a box of crayons. Somehow they slipped from her grasp. Broken crayons went flying over the floor. The jar of paste hit a corner of the table and crashed, sending splinters of glass and the sticky mess of paste everywhere.

When Mrs. Face arrived, Janet was in tears. Together they cleaned up the mess and then had a minute of prayer. Mrs. Face was a perceptive teacher and the prayer was not for forgiveness but was a sharing of difficulties. "Help us to do better," she concluded.

We cannot expect a child to feel that he has sinned when he did not mean to do wrong. He makes mistakes; matters get out of control sometimes—these are times to ask for help. Sin is when we *are* wrong. We often express this condition by doing wrong things, wanting to do them again. Sin is not causing trouble for an adult by error.

77

Marilyn teased the baby until he cried. She knew it was wrong, but she did it anyway. Her nature at that moment was sinful. She sinned when she put her selfish desires ahead of the baby's interests. If we keep these distinctions clear, we will be more helpful to children.

Stages of prayer

We not only teach children what prayer is, but how to pray. One helpful method is to think of prayer in stages:

1. First, we prepare for prayer. We think about God. With small children it will help to have a picture which will make them think of God. Talk about the picture. If it is a picture of Jesus with the children, help the children to see Jesus as a loving person, one who loves children. The children look happy with him. God loves us, too.

2. Think about God as being here now. What does he do for us? What has he given us?

3. What do we want to tell him? Praise him for his goodness. Love him for his love. Thank him for the world, for friends.

4. Ask God what he wants us to do. What does he want to tell us?

After we feel close to God, it is only natural that we will share our problems, our worries, our fears with him. We do not rush into God's presence as with a shopping list and a large basket. Conversation with a person you love is quiet, deep, enduring, unselfish.

Forms of prayer

For all people, the spontaneous prayer should be the most natural, a welling up of loving words at the time some incident calls for them. The child can learn to make new sentence prayers as well as to pray in words he has memorized.

As the child grows, he finds the world of prayer opening

many avenues to him. There are many forms his prayers can take. He can put his prayer into a sentence, or he can write a more complex prayer that will express his feelings and then use that prayer at a later time.

Eight-year-old Lennie was so full of mischief that his teacher spent a good deal of time keeping him within reasonable limits. At the moment the group was busy with their vacation church school workbooks and Lennie was bent over his workbook, writing firmly. When his teacher read the prayer Lennie wrote, she thought she would never again be impatient with him. "Thank you, God, for all the fun in the world." Certainly this was Lennie's own prayer, expressing his own values.

The child's idea of the world of prayer can grow as he realizes that prayer can express the feelings and thoughts of a group, not only of one individual. The Lord's Prayer is a group prayer. The experience of writing a prayer with others in his class helps the child realize that Christians often pray together.

Writing a litany is a good way to learn group praying. A litany is a responsive prayer. The dominant mood for the prayer is determined by the response. A prayer of thanksgiving might have the response "We thank thee, O Lord." A prayer of petition frequently has the response "We ask thee to hear us, O Lord."

As the harvest season approached, Miss Mays hoped her class of third-graders would feel thankful to God for the season's blessings. She began to set the stage by encouraging the children to put up pictures of harvest scenes in their room. She brought a bouquet of fall flowers. She helped the children think of the laden orchards along the highways, the fruit markets piled high with fruits and vegetables, the piles of pumpkins. As the children noted all these signs of God's care, their minds turned to ways of saying thank you.

"We could write a prayer," said Tony.

"What would we say?" asked Debbie. "We could say 'we thank you God,' and then put down what we thank him for."

"Could we, Miss Mays?" asked Charles.

"I think we could. If you tell me the things you are thankful for, I could write them on the chalkboard."

So Miss Mays wrote across the board "We thank you, God." The children began to list their reasons for thankfulness. "For yellow pumpkins," "blue grapes," "red apples," "for hickory nuts," came the first answers.

Charles said, "For seeds for the birds this winter."

Lois added, "And acorns that the squirrels will eat."

Jimmy thought of something beside food, "For the wood that's piled on our front porch for the fireplace," and the other children thought of warm homes.

Lois went back to food. "For the berries that grew this summer that our mothers put in the freezers."

Tony said, "How about being thankful for mothers and fathers? They get this stuff for us to eat."

Debbie said, "They buy the food with money the fathers get at their jobs. Can we thank God for money, and for jobs?"

By the time they were finished the chalkboard was filled with things they thanked God for. A little group editing erased ideas that were too much alike. Then the group tried reading the litany they had made. Tony read the reason and the group responded "We thank you, God."

"I hate to see our prayer erased," said Linda.

Miss Mays said, "I'll copy it down and, if you'd like, I'll have copies made so each of you can have your own copy."

"We can take them home and use them with our families," suggested Tony.

"You know what?" said Charles. "The prayer we wrote is something like the one we pray in church. The minister says what we pray for and we sing 'Lord, have mercy.'"

Collects

Having written prayers of their own, the boys and girls are ready to appreciate the prayers other people have written. They have already had some experience in using written prayers in the service of the church. Much of the wealth of prayer in the church is in the form of collects. These are short expressions of one idea. Collects are always addressed to God. They usually give the reason why the petitioner feels it is appropriate to approach God, have a petition, a reason for the petition, and a conclusion. Some are difficult, but others can be grasped and used by children as their own prayers.

The structure of collects

The child may be helped to understand and appreciate the formal prayers, or collects, of the church if he can see the outline on which they are built. Consider the Collect for Peace, used in the Vespers Service:

ADDRESS	O God,
REASON FOR ASKING THIS PETITION	from whom all holy desires, all good counsels, and all just works do proceed:
PETITION	Give unto thy servants that peace which the world cannot give;
EFFECT DESIRED	that our hearts may be set to obey thy commandments, and also that by thee, we, being defended from the fear of our enemies, may pass our time in rest and quietness;
CONCLU-SION	through the merits of Jesus Christ our Savior, who liveth and reigneth with thee and the Holy Ghost, one God, world without end. Amen.

This sequence of ideas is typical of almost all collects. Once mastered, prayers are easily made up by using this pattern.

Hymns are prayers

Many hymns are prayers and should be so understood. The young school-age child soon learns to sing "Father, We Thank Thee for the Night," and if he is directed to the meaning of the words, he will use it as a prayer of thanksgiving.

When he is a little older he will find a vehicle for his prayer in a hymn like:

Teach me, my God and King,
In all things thee to see,
And what I do in anything,
To do it as for thee.

We can sing hymns as prayers, or read the words for greater emphasis on the meaning. Sometimes playing the music of a familiar hymn will help to create an atmosphere in which prayer is natural. This use of hymn tunes is a good way to prepare the group for worship or prayer.

Some Bible passages are prayers

Near the end of King David's life he called together the leaders and mighty men of the nation and told them of his plans for the country. Solomon was to be the next king and build a great temple to the Lord. At this time of great national decision, before the whole assembly, David prayed:

> "Blessed are thou, O Lord, the God of Israel our father for ever and ever. Thine, O Lord, is the greatness, and the power, and the glory, and the victory, and the majesty; for all that is in the heavens and in the earth is thine; thine is the kingdom, O Lord, and thou art exalted as head above all. Both riches and honor come from thee, and thou rulest over all. In thy hand are power and might; and in thy hand it is to make great and to give strength to all. And now we thank thee, our God, and praise thy glorious name" (*1 Chronicles 29:10-13*).

We are not kings, nor making decisions of national importance, and yet David's prayer can be our own as we think of the greatness of God and of our dependence on him for every blessing. If you read further in this chapter, you find one of the most familiar of our offering prayers: "For all things come from thee, and of thy own have we given thee."

The Bible contains many prayers that we can use and make our own as we enter into the experience of the writer. A great many of the Psalms are prayers. Think of Psalm 51, one of the great prayers of confession. We use parts of it as an offertory in The Service, "Create in me a clean heart, O God." Or think of a prayer of praise, like Psalm 145: "I will extol thee, my God and King, and bless thy name for ever and ever."

People who wrote prayers

Miss Francis had placed on the browsing table a book of prayers by Robert Louis Stevenson. Fred looked over the table and picked up the book.

"Stevenson? That's not the one who wrote *Kidnapped* and *Treasure Island*, is it?"

"Yes it is. And he wrote a whole book of prayers!"

Fred took the book over to a corner and began to look at it.

Sometimes children can learn a great deal about prayer by knowing something about the circumstances under which prayers were written, or the people who prayed them.

Fifth-graders had been studying about great Christians. Reading prayers written by these heroes gave them new insights into the place prayer has in the Christian life. Polycarp was a second-century Christian who gave his life for his faith. To read "We pray for all saints, for kings and rulers, for the enemies of the Cross of Christ" against this background knowledge helped the boys and girls understand what it means to pray for those who persecute you. Even when the prayer was one that the children could not make their own and use in their own worship, they had a feeling of sharing the experience of another Christian and understanding that prayer played an important part in his life.

Memorizing

Should we teach children to memorize prayers? The first usefulness is the convenience of having prayers at times when we cannot have them written down, or when it is not feasible to create them. We memorize table graces since we are more likely to use them if we do not need to hunt one up in a book or think out in advance what we want to pray. The Lord's Prayer is used in so many of our group meetings that it is convenient to have it memorized.

Of course, the values of memorization are completely lost if children have memorized the wrong words. Gertrude, who memorized "partly do we repent" certainly did not have in her possession either the words or the import of the prayer her teacher thought she had learned. Even with the Lord's Prayer, which we all "know," it is well to check to see that children are really praying the right words. There is no value, either, in memorizing prayers we do not understand at all. Most of us, as adults, continue to find new depths of meaning in the Lord's Prayer as the experiences of life bring new illumination to it. Of course, children cannot have the depth of comprehension they will have later on, but they should understand the words and appreciate the prayer at their own level of comprehension.

The child will probably memorize a prayer like the Lord's Prayer from repeated use, without being particularly conscious that he is memorizing. But study is needed if he is to memorize it accurately and with understanding.

Miss Virdon's children were studying the Collect for Peace used in Vespers:

O God, from whom all holy desires . . .

Nothing in the vocabulary or ideas of the prayer was beyond these sixth-graders. "Who wrote it?" asked Dennis. No one knew, so they went to the church library for help.

Marian found information about the prayer in Dr. Luther Reed's book *The Lutheran Liturgy* and reported back to the class. "It's a very old prayer of the church," she said. "It was used long before Luther's time. It was written in Latin in the latter half of the fifth-century—that's after A.D. 450. It was a time when people certainly felt they needed to pray for peace. There was fighting everywhere. The Huns and the Vandals were attacking Rome and it seemed as if the whole world would be destroyed by the wars."

"Boy, they should have heard about the atomic bomb," said Dennis.

"I guess the Huns and Vandals seemed just as bad as the bomb to them," Larry remarked.

"Luther translated the prayer into German," Marian continued. "And it's used by Catholics and Episcopalians and Lutherans all around the world."

"It fits right into our time," said Dennis, "because we know what 'fear of our enemies' means."

"But the prayer is more than just 'please defend us from the atom bomb,'" said Jean. "It's talking about inside peace, too. It's not only peace from war, but peace in our hearts because we obey God."

These sixth-graders had reached an understanding of the collect which enabled them to use it as their own. They used it in their worship. Dennis suggested that it would be a good prayer to have around.

"We might print it on a card and put it up on our mirrors at home, or in our wallets," he said. The class liked his idea and made prayer cards with this collect. By the time they had studied the prayer, used it in worship, and printed it on cards, they had memorized the prayer without trying.

What are the results?

What do we hope to achieve by instruction in prayer? An understanding by the child of what prayer is, and a desire to enjoy it. But even more, we are leading to a habit that will bring the child into natural conversation with God. We want him to know and to practice prayer at any time, at any place. We want his life to be illuminated by both the quick reaching out to God in times of need or gladness and by formal times of prayer in which heart and mind work together to sustain this conversation.

Learning hymns

"We'll sing," Phil looked at his notes, "the hymn 'Let Us, with a Gladsome Mind.'"

The pianist played. A weak murmur half lifted from the children.

"Can't you sing better than that?" asked Phil.

What was wrong? The hymn had been carefully chosen. It fitted into the worship theme; it gave expression to the children's feeling of praise for God.

It was a fine hymn, but the children had never heard the words or tune before. They were unable to sing it because they did not know it. They needed instruction in the hymn. The worship period was not the time to learn the hymn; that should have been cared for earlier. How often we have expected children to use hymns worshipfully when they could not even sing them!

Small children learn their songs by rote, hearing them sung over and over. Sometimes children need to learn to listen. They may be singing a droning kind of tune instead of the song, simply because they have not understood what singing a song is like. You may need to help the child get the idea that music goes up and down to make a tune. Try singing the scale—do, re, mi, fa, so, la, ti, do—using gestures to indicate that each note goes up, up, up. It's like going up a flight of stairs. Then ask the children to listen carefully to the tune of the new song to see how those notes go up and go down. Sometimes this is all children need to grasp the idea.

Children in Grades 1 and 2 are not ready to read music, but they can be helped with a song chart on which the words of the song are written in large enough letters so that all can read them. (The hymnal for the prereading children gives helps to the teacher.) With children of this age begin by listening to the music, then humming along, then singing "la-la" to the tune. After they are familiar with the tune you are ready to try the words. Read the words together, making sure the children know the meaning of every word and thought. Now you are ready to try singing words to music. If there still seems to be difficulty, ask the children to listen again while you sing the words to the music, then have them sing with you.

Children in third grade and above can use their own hymnal, although in learning a new song it may be helpful to have the words written on a chalkboard where all can see and still follow the leader's directions. (There is a hymnal for Grades 1 through 6.) The process of listening, singing "la-la," then saying the words together before singing matching words and tune is good for children of this age, too. You may wish to have these older children learn something about simple time if this has not been done elsewhere. Time in the music they will sing is based on the count of 1, 2, 3, 4. A whole note counts 4; a half note, 2; a quarter note, 1. That is, we can express the count of four by one whole note, two half notes, or four quarter notes. If we know this, we can get some of the rhythm of a new hymn.

> One whole note (𝆶)   = 4 counts
> Two half notes (𝆷 𝆷)   = 4 counts
> Four quarter notes (𝅘𝅥 𝅘𝅥 𝅘𝅥 𝅘𝅥)= 4 counts

Learning to sing a hymn in this way is just a beginning. If we really want to know a hymn there is much more we will want to learn. We will find out the general meaning of the hymn. Is it a hymn of praise or a prayer for help? Why did the writer write it? Does it express his faith in God or his thankfulness for God's gifts? Is he telling a story? Here are some hymn types:

STORY	*While Shepherds Watched Their Flocks by Night*
PRAISE	*Holy, Holy, Holy, Lord God Almighty*
FAITH IN GOD'S LOVE	*God, Who Made the Earth*
PRAYER FOR HELP	*Jesus, Friend of Little Children*
THANKFULNESS	*Now Thank We All Our God*
PRAYER FOR OTHERS	*Remember All the People*
HELP IN BEING GOOD	*Teach Me, My God and King*

Some hymns are more interesting to us when we know something about the writer or composer, or the conditions under which the hymn was written. "A Mighty Fortress" gains in meaning when we know that Martin Luther wrote it when he was defying the whole Roman church and Empire. Hymns by Charles Wesley are even more interesting when we know of the writer's devotion to Christ. Sometimes it is well to introduce a hymn by telling a story about it, or to combine the learning of the words and music with stories about it. The new hymnals will be of help in this area, too.

6

Resources for Worship

"THIS is the first time I've ever planned worship," said Lennie. "What do we do?"

"Start by choosing a Bible reading," answered Myrna.

"That's right," Lennie agreed. "We always read from the Bible, don't we?"

"Oh yes," said Myrna.

"Why?" Lennie asked.

How would you answer Lennie? The Bible is woven into our worship. It is the chief treasure and heritage of the church. In our private or family devotions we read parts of it. The Service of the church is derived from the Bible. Our worship in the church schools is based on Bible reading.

THE BIBLE

The Bible is central in our worship because in it we hear God speaking to us. The Bible is a record of God's dealings with men—men typical enough of all mankind so that God's relation to them is much like his relation to us. In the law and prophets, in history and poetry, and especially in Jesus, we hear the Word of God.

Then, too, the Bible's style of presentation and beautiful phrasing has been a source of inspiration and beauty for generations of Christians. Our church liturgies are enriched by the use of Bible language. That language enables us to share two thousand years of Christian experience and thou-

Joanne Dunyan
Grade 1

My sister and I praying

"What the Almighty can do"   David Bayer—Grade 5

sands more of Hebrew background. It enables us to choose the best thinking and most beautiful literature from an important portion of the history of mankind. We cannot do without the Bible in our worship. But in order to get the most out of it, we must use it with understanding.

Understanding

The fourth-graders had been studying about Moses for several Sundays. In the worship at the close of the unit Marjorie read Deuteronomy 31:1-6, which contains the words Moses spoke to the people at the end of his life. Moses' reference to the past had meaning for the group because they had studied about it. "Be strong and of good courage, do not fear or be in dread of them: for it is the LORD your God who goes with you; he will not fail you or forsake you." When Marjorie read these words of Moses the group saw them as the expression of a man they had learned to admire. They knew that Moses could say these words because he had lived so close to God. The words meant more because the boys and girls had the necessary background to understand. All our Bible study—in the church schools, in church, at home—contributes to our understanding of the Bible as we use it in worship.

The class had been studying about Saul, a king who failed. Larry opened his workbook very slowly, as if he had something on his mind. He kept silent while the group discussed the reasons King Saul found it hard to obey God. When they came to the question "What are some things that sometimes make it hard for you to obey God?" he bent his head still lower over the page and became absorbed in his hands.

Suddenly he looked up. "I can tell you one thing," he blurted out. "When you know you are disobeying God, you feel awful. You feel as if there was nobody real."

The other boys and girls looked startled. Did Larry ever feel like this? They began to talk about the sadness of feeling separated from God by disobedience. A genuine regret for doing wrong and a desire to be close to God permeated all the worship that day. The class had been prepared for this desire by study and discussion. In return, the worship heightened the value of the study. Miss Francis realized that the worship had helped the group to achieve the objectives of the unit in a way that discussion and study alone could not have done. Out of experiences like this boys and girls learn to appreciate the Bible as a book not only to be studied but to be loved.

"Did you realize that the Psalms were hymns?" said sixth-grade Dan to Mrs. Law. "And that the people sang some of them on their way to Jerusalem?"

Mrs. Law nodded and listened as Dan went on to tell her what he had just read. She watched Dan's new use of the Psalms during worship. They had come alive to him because he understood better how they had been written and used.

Tim and Wendy stayed after class to talk with Mrs. Bailey about plans for the next session.

"I'll read the Bible," said Tim. "We've chosen Jeremiah 31:31-34. This word 'covenant' comes up again and again, Mrs. Bailey. Do you think everybody will know what it means?"

"Probably not, Tim."

"Well, then, maybe I ought to explain it. But not right in the worship period. Hey, could I write it on the chalkboard before class? Then everyone could see it."

"That's a good idea, Tim," Mrs. Bailey agreed.

"Something puzzles me," said Wendy. "It says here, 'my covenant which they broke, though I was their husband.' What does that mean?"

"Again and again the prophets refer to the relation between Israel and God as being like that of husband and wife. God had chosen Israel and loved and cared for her as a husband cares for his wife. In return the people of Israel owed God love and faithfulness, as a wife owes it to her husband," Mrs. Bailey answered.

"Oh, I see," said Wendy. "Tim, how are you going to explain that to the kids?"

Not all parts of the Bible are within the comprehension of children, and this comprehension varies with the age. As a general rule, teachers will be most successful in using the Bible in worship if they use those parts suggested in the lesson materials. There they have the help of people who have given considerable thought to the parts of the Bible selected for study. Educators worked out a plan for the overall program. The writers of the materials thought long and hard about the Bible sections used. Their ideas were weighed by editors and age-group specialists. The passages selected for each age group should be suitable.

When a teacher chooses parts of the Bible to use, the main standard is that he must present to the children a true picture of God. With young children the emphasis should always be on God's love. This is not because God's judgment is not valid and a necessary part of the picture, but because the small child is just building his picture of God. If we emphasize God's judgment or wrath, the child will think that wrath is the outstanding characteristic of God. God's outstanding characteristic in his dealings with man is his faithful love and desire to win back the sinner.

Ways of using the Bible in worship

The most common use of the Bible in worship is simple reading. The teacher reads a verse or a story to the small children. An older child reads aloud a designated passage.

But the Bible isn't really used if it is not heard, even though it is read aloud. Children should learn to read it well, so that those listening may hear and understand the words. Muffled reading, mispronounced words, reading that is too rapid or not loud enough—all these work against the listener. This should be explained to children who read, so that they will see the reason for practicing and preparing to read even one small verse.

Children too young to grasp a story in the words of the Bible should be told the story in words they do understand. Even here it is wise for the teacher to have the Bible open on her lap and explain that the story she is telling comes from the Bible.

Listening is important, too. Teachers can help the children learn to listen creatively.

"Let's close our eyes," said Miss Thomas to her fourth-graders. "I'm going to read some poetry from the Bible. I want you to make pictures with your mind as I read these words. Try to see what the poet is describing. I'll make a few words easier for you."

She read from Psalm 104.

"*Out there [Yonder] is the sea, great and wide,*
   filled [which teems] with more things than we
      can count [innumerable],
   living things both small and great.
There go the ships,
   and the whale [Leviathan] which thou didst
      form to play [sport] in it."

"What pictures do you see?"

Ronnie usually had very little to say, but now his face lighted up.

"You walk along the beach in the early morning," said Ronnie, "and you see—oh, everything! 'More than we can count,'" he repeated with satisfaction. "Blobs of jelly fish, and tiny crabs, and shells that the waves brought in. Sometimes they're alive, but not often, because the waves just roll in the shells after the animal is gone. But one time I saw lots and lots of tiny shells—coquinas they are called—and they were alive, because all at once those tiny shells stood on end and began to burrow down in the sand! And if you wade out in the water you see little fish swimming around, and once I saw a whole school of dolphins farther out. They play around . . . ."

"*O Lord, how very many [manifold] are thy works!*" read Miss Thomas softly.

"*In wisdom hast thou made them all;*
the earth is full of thy creatures."

Sometimes a psalm is read effectively when the group reads responsively, especially if the reading is planned so that idea balances idea.

Under is the sea, great and wide, which teems with things innumerable,

RESPONSE: *living things both small and great.*

There go the ships,

RESPONSE: *and Leviathan which thou didst form to sport in it.*

Sometimes a story gains in impact if it is read as a drama. The story of the healing of the paralytic (*Matthew 9:1-8*) can be used if one child reads the narrative parts, others read the words of the scribes, another Jesus' words.

From this kind of reading it is only another step to simple dramatizations of Bible stories. These can be effective presentations of God's Word if they are done simply and with careful consideration of their meaning.

Choral reading

"We're going to try something new," said Pamela as the other girls and boys came in. "Miss Clendennon says she'll help us. It's choral reading."

"Choral reading?" said Chuck. "What's that?"

"Some people call it a speech choir," Pamela replied.

"But a choir sings," Chuck said quickly.

"And a speech choir speaks," answered Pam. "Speaking voices sound nice, too. First we decide who has dark voices and who has light."

"Does your voice match your hair?" asked Chuck. "That's good! Does your voice match your hair?" He laughed.

Pam paid no attention. "Come on. Let's try out. Don, you say something. Say 'God is our refuge and strength.' Come on, say it."

Don coughed, then said the words.

"What do you kids think? Would you call that light or dark? Dark voices are lower and deeper."

"Dark," said Jinny.

"O.K. Don, you're dark. Jinny, you try it . . . ."

"Dark," said Sandra and Jill. By this time the other boys and girls were becoming interested. They stopped fooling and listened as each one tried out. In a little while everyone had been placed in a group: boys, light; boys, dark; girls, light; girls, dark.

With Miss Clendennon's help the group read together the first part of Psalm 46, which they had been studying. They talked about its meaning, told how it made them feel, then read the verses in unison.

"Which group should read the first two lines?" Miss Clendennon asked.

They tried it various ways and finally Chuck said, "Those are the most important words in the psalm. I think we should all say them together."

The class tried the verses in unison and decided it was the best way to express what the lines meant. Then they tried the next lines in various combinations.

"Maybe one voice saying 'There is a river whose streams make glad the city of God' would call attention to the lines," said Jill. "It's a kind of far-off dream, it seems to me."

"Let's try it," Sandra suggested, and they did. They liked the variety of a solo voice for those lines. It seemed to bring out a different quality.

Then the group read through the psalm with each section taking the parts assigned.

"Not bad," said Chuck, "but should it be said this way all at one speed? Maybe some parts should be slower or faster."

"How do we decide?" Jill asked.

"By trying them out," said Pam. Reading aloud, listening, considering, finally the group worked out the tempo of each line.

"Let's use this in our worship," Chuck suggested. "Maybe we should memorize it—say! We don't need to! We know it already!"

The group had memorized the psalm without consciously trying to do so, for they had studied it and repeated it until it was a part of them.

Choral reading can be a worshipful use of Bible materials. Each child feels that he is taking part in a group activity. He understands the meaning of the passage used and enters into its feeling.

Using the Bible with hymns

Sometimes Bible material and hymns can be used together to add to the effectiveness of both. The Twenty-Third Psalm can be read in connection with a hymn based on it, such as "The King of Love My Shepherd Is." The repetition in two different forms deepens both impressions.

Another illustration is the connection between Psalm 46 and Luther's hymn "A Mighty Fortress Is Our God."

Using the Bible with art

After Miss Thomas' boys and girls had read and listened to part of Psalm 104 about the sea, they began to draw the pictures they had seen in their minds. Some children who find it hard to put their feelings into words can express them well in pictures. Sally was this kind. She had said nothing during the discussion, but when the class began to draw, her sketch of the rolling waves, with shells on the shore and the suggestion of a dolphin frisking in the distance, conveyed the feeling of joy in God's wonderful world.

"Let's put Sally's picture at the worship center," said Ronnie. "It will make everything clearer when we worship."

Before Christmas the first-graders had been working on a mural of the manger scene. Miss Groat had fastened the paper to the wall at opposite corners of the room. Her first-graders soon were busy with their crayons. In the center of the picture they drew the baby Jesus and his mother. On one side were the shepherds with their sheep. On the other were the wise men with their camels. There were lots of animals in the picture.

When the mural was finished, Paul sat back to look at it. "Let's worship right in front of our picture," he said. "We can pretend we are right in the Christmas stable."

THE HYMNALS

On your reference shelf of resources for worship, stand the hymnals of our church—the *Service Book and Hymnal,* the prereading hymnal for use in the church school with children who cannot read well as yet, and the *Church School Hymnal for Children* for use with children of grade-school age, especially those who can read. (The teacher of second-grade pupils has a choice of hymnals, therefore.)

Children in Grade 2 and under find the use of hymnals difficult, as the complications of following words in a book and trying to sing at the same time are beyond many of them. The children's hymnal for this age does not expect the child to have his own book. The hymnal will be a guide for leaders, and the child will learn to sing the hymns by hearing them, or in some cases, by using a song chart.

The *Church School Hymnal for Children* is designed for the child in grade school, but is most helpful from third grade on. This hymnal is attractively illustrated in a way the child will enjoy. He will like using it. A leader's guide provides background information as well as helps in teaching and interpreting the hymns.

Why use hymns in worship?

Hymns and music play an important role in worship generally, and certainly in the Lutheran church. Of course, it is possible to worship without music; the Suffrages are planned this way. But singing offers many advantages. The praise that we would speak otherwise in hushed, awkward words we can sing joyously, without restraint in "Praise to the Lord, the Almighty, the King of Creation."

Thanksgiving that sounds stifled and inept bursts forth with satisfying words and tones as we sing "Now thank we all our God with heart and hands and voices."

Confessions that we hardly know how to make find their outlet in the words " 'Twas I, Lord Jesus, I it was denied thee" in the hymn "Ah, Holy Jesus, How Hast Thou Offended."

Petitions that, without the help of hymns, might stay on the low level of personal needs rise to prayers for the kingdom as we sing "Lord, Keep Us Steadfast in Thy Word."

And dedication and resolve become deeper and more meaningful as we express our feelings in hymns like "Teach Me, My God and King."

Hymns affect our feeling and mood. Who has not experienced a lift of heart when he joins a congregation in singing "Beautiful Savior"?

The triumphant gladness of Easter morning is never felt more keenly than when we sing "Jesus Christ is risen today, Alleluia."

Whatever the load of personal care and worry, taking part in singing this hymn helps the Christian share in Easter joy.

Using the hymns of the church helps us to feel a part of that world-wide, timeless fellowship of the saints. Whether it is the Negro spiritual "Were You There When They Crucified My Lord?" or a hymn of the ancient Greek church like "Come, Ye Faithful, Raise the Strain," or a medieval Latin carol like "Good Christian Men, Rejoice," or a French carol like "Angels We Have Heard on High," we know that we are united with those of other nations, other races, other centuries, as we share the Christian experience that produced the hymn and the faith that keeps it alive.

There are overtones in good hymns that help us to change our wrong attitudes and strengthen our weak inclinations. They help us to feel a strength and steadiness of belief in the God who rules over history that an argument in words could not produce.

Learning precedes use

We have discussed simple ways of teaching a hymn to children in the classroom. They should learn the tune so that they can sing it with pleasure. They should understand the ideas of the hymn. Any obscure words should be explained.

Some hymns that we use with children need study before they can be understood. "O Come, O Come, Emmanuel" is one of these. It needs study, but it is worth it, for it conveys a sense of the mystery of God's dealings with men.

This mystery is an essential part of our religious experience. The hymn is worth study, too, because it helps us to feel our continuity with the past, not only with the medieval Christians who used the prayers on which it is based, but also with the Old Testament people who stood at the base of Mount Sinai and who longed for the coming of a Redeemer.

There are some adult hymns that children need to learn because they are an important part of our heritage. We recognize that the child does not find "A Mighty Fortress Is Our God" easy to sing or to comprehend, but the hymn is such an important part of our Protestant and Lutheran heritage that he ought to know it.

Many hymns will mean more to the child if he knows something about their background. This is especially true of older children, who begin to get an idea of their relation to the past.

The children had learned to sing "All Creatures of Our God and King." Miss Skinner had helped them to see the pictures behind the words so that they enjoyed the hymn. But after they associated the poem with Francis of Assisi, whose life story they had studied, the hymn gained new gleams of brilliance. It was not only a fine hymn, but an expression of a personality they had learned to admire.

In the same way, the picture of Charles Wesley writing "Ye Servants of God, Your Master Proclaim," "to be sung in a tumult," added depth and meaning to the hymn. The poem was not just brave words; it is an expression of a man who had literally sung in a tumult, when men were pelting him with stones and curses.

Judging a hymn

Only good hymns are good enough to use with children, but sometimes we are puzzled about choosing the good. The hymns in your children's hymnals passed many tests as to merit and fitness before they were included. Feel safe in using these books. But you may want to know how to judge hymns for yourself.

"What's wrong with the B-I-B-L-E song?" asked a teacher. "The children like to sing it."

We consider first of all a hymn's worth and merit. It is very difficult to say why the music of one song is good and the music of another, poor. But speaking only of music for hymns, we can say that a good hymn tune produces in the singer effects that help him to worship. A poor tune brings to his mind unworshipful attitudes, make him think of sentimental love songs or warlike shouts, or simply plays on emotions and never leads to worship and reverence. A good hymn tune will have quiet dignity without being stuffy, or it will be lively and joyous without being raucous, or it will be stately without being overly dramatic. It will inspire without being frenzied. It will be beautiful, not shallow, sticky sweet, or of passing fancy.

We can be more definite when we add that the music of the hymns should be singable, within the range of children's voices, and with a melodic pattern that children can learn.

It is easier to set up standards for judging the words of a hymn. They should be sensible. The words of songs like "The B-I-B-L-E," or "Wonderful Words of Life" really are not sensible. They do not say anything. This lack of sense is permissible in fun songs, but not in worship. Words and music should fit so that they can be sung together. The religious ideas of the poem-hymn should be acceptable.

The child is learning as he sings. He is absorbing ideas about God; he is developing an attitude toward God and the church that is strongly influenced by the songs he sings. He may be more affected by the hymns than by any other part of your teaching. As he sings a hymn, he is participating, perhaps to a greater degree than in a discussion. This participation keenly influences him.

The ideas learned through singing hymns are often those people remember best. You will remember that Luther's enemies were particularly disturbed at the way his hymns swept the country, teaching people his doctrines as they sang the songs. Examine a fine hymn like "O Worship the King." Note how true to our faith are the ideas expressed there. God is our King. . . . Sing his wonderful love. . . . The Almighty has made the earth. . . . his bountiful care. . . . We are frail, but can trust God's unfailing goodness. . . . our Maker, Defender, Redeemer, and Friend.

We should avoid religious songs that express wrong ideas or wrong attitudes. Some of the sentimental songs are offensive in their chumminess. God is not a sweetheart! Neither is he "the man upstairs," whose help we can command.

To sum up, some of the criteria on which we judge a hymn to be good for children are these:

1. The music is such that the child can sing it.
2. The music helps his worshipful mood.
3. The words make sense.
4. The child can understand them.
5. The ideas are within the child's grasp, or can be explained to him.
6. The ideas are true to Christian experience and Lutheran doctrine. They do not contradict or undermine the Christian idea of God.
7. The hymn has lasting beauty.

We must judge hymns, too, on their usefulness as tools, as aids to worship. We must choose those which will help the particular children with whom we are working. Hymns must be suitable to the age group. This does not mean that, with older children, we will not introduce some hymns that are more adult in their ideas, if the hymn is one that is important in our Christian worship and tradition. Perhaps an illustration will help to make the distinction clear.

"Rock of Ages" is an adult hymn that is not usable with children, even with much explanation. The ideas are too difficult for the child to grasp. The symbolism of a rock being Jesus Christ is a hurdle the child cannot surmount. But "Built on a Rock the Church Doth Stand" is an adult hymn that can be used with children if it is explained. The use of a rock as a symbol in this hymn is one that children, with help, can grasp, because the rock acts like a rock and remains one. The figure, "We are God's house of living stones," is one that most children will not grasp, but the idea it expresses is not the entire hymn. It is pictured in other ways they can comprehend. In other words, the child will not understand all of this hymn, but he will understand enough of it so that it will have meaning for him. "Rock of Ages," however, is built in its entirety on a complex symbol.

We choose hymns, too, for their usefulness in the particular time of worship. What do we expect the hymn to do? To convey what ideas? Suggest what mood? How does the hymn fit into the plans for worship, so that the occasion will be a unified one? How does the hymn help to achieve the objectives of the unit or session?

Mrs. Burgess had underlined the objective "To help the child think of the Bible as a way through which we come to know God and what he has done for us." How was this to be accomplished? She studied her lesson plan carefully. Something more was needed. If they followed the suggestion of using the hymn "Rejoice, the Lord is King" for worship it would reinforce the ideas of the rest of the session. If, in getting ready for worship, she could help the children see how the ideas of Psalm 100 were linked with the hymn, the impression of learning to know God through the Bible would be even stronger.

Ways of using hymns

Singing. Has not our chief acquaintance with hymns been made through group singing? The Lutheran tradition of congregational singing is strong, and at church schools we sing hymns together as an essential part of our worship. Singing offers the individual a way to express his own worship and at the same time share worship with others. But it is not the only way to sing hymns.

Patty had a part in the Christmas worship. She was to place the shepherds in the manger scene. She waited patiently while other second-graders placed the figures of the holy family in the stable. Then Mrs. Savage, one of the choir members, began to sing "What Child Is This?" Patty placed the shepherds outside the stable and stood there, looking at the scene. The stable seemed to grow and grow until Patty felt as if she were present at the stable in Bethlehem. Using the hymn as a solo impressed her because it was unusual and appropriate. It also helped introduce her to a hymn she had not sung before.

Some hymns lend themselves to dramatic forms. Try the familiar Christmas hymn "While Shepherds Watched Their Flocks by Night" with a solo voice singing the angel's words, and the group singing the narrative parts. The hymn story becomes more vivid in this way.

The fifth-graders were planning worship. They intended to use the hymn "Come, Together Let Us Sing."

"Seems sort of silly," said Freddie, "for everybody to sing 'Come, together let us sing.' That's what we're doing."

"How else would you do it?" asked Janet.

"I'm not sure. Maybe some of us could sing those first four lines and then everybody could sing the last two. That way we'd notice what the hymn really says. The first bunch would be saying, 'Come, let's praise God by singing,' and everybody would do just that—'Praise to God in highest heaven, And on earth be glory given.' I think we'd feel the hymn more that way."

The class tried singing the hymn as Freddie had suggested and they did 'feel the hymn more' as he had said.

Reading the words. A hymn is also a poem. How often our minds slide away from the words we are singing. Reading them aloud will help us realize what the hymn is saying. It focuses our attention on the meaning rather than the sound. "Teach Me, My God and King" is a poem that can be used as a prayer by reading the words as well as singing them. "What Can I Give Him?" is an appropriate prayer for the offering, whether sung or spoken.

On the other hand, the music of the hymn tune can be used without words as a prelude to worship. It is a gracious way of saying that it is time to put away other concerns, to become quiet so that we can worship.

In judging a hymn, the most important point is none of these things we have mentioned, but whether our singing of it will please God. The primary use of hymns is to please him.

Using art forms. Another way of enriching hymn study is by illustrating a hymn. This activity accomplishes a careful study of the meaning of the words, since we have to understand what we are to illustrate. It helps the child to perceive the mood and tone of the hymn, as well. "All Things Bright and Beautiful" would almost certainly call for the pictures suggested by the words—flowers, birds, purple mountains, rivers, sunsets, winter wind and summer sun, ripe fruits in the garden. If the group were also illustrating "I Sing the Mighty Power of God," they would see that both hymns praise God the Maker of the world, but from different angles. The second hymn summons pictures of great seas and vast galaxies in space, the sun and moon and stars.

These illustrations may be used in making posters about a

hymn, or in making hymn cards with the words of the hymn written on them.

The meaning of the hymns may be interpreted by drawings. In this case the actual word pictures of the hymn would not be emphasized so much as the way it made the child feel. For example, the happy feelings arising from "Beautiful Savior" might be interpreted in a picture showing children bringing flowers to Jesus as a sign of their love. The picture would have no basis in the actual words of the hymn but rather in the feelings of the child.

Making a background for a hymn can strengthen its appeal. The third-graders had worked on a wall drawing showing the Nativity scene. "Let's sing in front of our picture," said Ann. So they arranged their chairs in an arc before their picture and sang "Come, All Ye Shepherds" to express their love for the baby Jesus.

Sometimes pictures or magazine illustrations can be used with hymns in similar ways. However, the children's own work is usually more significant to them.

Most of these activities are useful in a period when you are studying or preparing for a hymn rather than in worship itself.

The Service Book and Hymnal

On the shelf beside the Bible and the children's hymnals, the worker with children places the *Service Book and Hymnal*. It will not be used in worship with children perhaps as much as the other two books are, but it has many values for corporate and private worship. In it you will find a great amount of information that will help you. Information about the church year and the church calendar, the proper liturgical colors, and other items of this kind, may be useful to answer questions that the child may raise as he observes the conduct of his church.

Pages 280 to 283 contain tables of lessons and psalms for each Sunday of the year. These are often helpful in planning a worship for a particular day or season.

The Service is printed in its entirety in the first pages of the Service Book, where it can be referred to when there are questions about The Service or when there is an opportunity to study it.

The hymnal is the place to examine when interest in a hymn writer inspires a desire to know about his other hymns. Four of Martin Luther's hymns are in the children's hymnal, but the *Service Book and Hymnal* contains three additional ones which an interested boy or girl may wish to look up.

Beside information related to worship, the *Service Book and Hymnal* contains many resources to be used in worship. There are many additional hymns that might have a use in worship as poems.

> *God himself is present*
> *Let us now adore him,*

is a call to worship that could well express the sense of the mystery that God is the Ruler of the universe and at the same time present with each worshiper.

The *Service Book and Hymnal* offers a wealth of material for responsive readings. There is a large section of collects and prayers, and also the Suffrages, which are brief offices of worship. Obviously this material will not be used in classroom worship, for our worship is brief and should be related to the day's study. But the material contains a wealth of devotional help for the personal devotions of teacher and child.

Look, too, at the morning and evening prayers from Luther's *Small Catechism.*

Miss Schall's fifth-graders were disturbed. One of their classmates, Bonnie, had been ill all winter and now, in the early spring, had died. It was the children's first experience with the death of someone their own age whom they knew well. Talking about it seemed to help only a little. After a while Miss Schall opened the Service Book to the Burial Service and read the special prayer to be used at the burial of a child:

> "O God, whose most dear Son took little children into his arms and blessed them: Give us grace, we beseech thee, to entrust the soul of this child to thy never-failing care and love, and bring us all to thy heavenly kingdom; through the same thy Son, Jesus Christ our Lord. Amen."

"I guess we forgot that God would be there," said Doug, with evident comfort.

When certain material in the *Service Book and Hymnal* is suitable for use with children, there is an advantage in having them use this book, which can be of great help to them in their devotions as they grow more mature. Of course, its use in even this limited fashion should generally be with the older children, from fourth grade on, who can read well enough to find their way in it. But the younger ones can learn something just from seeing the book the grown-ups use.

SYMBOLISM

Dr. Franklin Clark Fry once told a story about a small child whose father, a soldier, had been away from home for a long time. Every night the mother showed the child a photograph, and explained that it was his father; and the child kissed it goodnight. Then soldier-father came home. The child was bewildered by this strange man who had suddenly come to take a large part of the mother's time and attention. He refused to have anything to do with him. At bedtime both parents took the child to his crib.

"This is your father, dear," said the mother. "Now come, kiss daddy goodnight."

The child broke loose from her, ran to the bureau, and picked up the photograph and kissed it. The symbol meant more to him than the person it stood for.

A symbol is important only because it points to reality. It is a visible sign for something else. It stands for or suggests something, as the national flag stands for our country. Some acts are symbolic, as when an audience stands as a sign of respect for a distinguished person, or claps as a sign of approval. Some symbols suggest the proper action, as a highway STOP sign suggests that we stop.

We use symbols because they are more vivid than words (although words, too, are symbols). They are shortcuts to meaning, as a road sign indicating a curve to the left is a quick way of indicating the way the road turns. Symbols express the "inexpressible"—as anyone knows who has stood at attention while the flag of his country is raised on its staff.

Although none of these symbols are religious, what we have said is true also of religious symbols. The cross reminds us of the Crucifixion, which itself represents God's saving love. When we kneel to pray our action is symbolic of humility before God. Religious symbols can tell us what to do. Someone says "Let us bow our heads"; we prepare to pray.

Religious symbols are of two kinds; the first reminds us of something we already know. The cross is a meaningful symbol to us because we already know about the Crucifixion.

The second kind of symbol points toward something not entirely expressible; it tries to give us information about something we cannot fully know. The term "Father" is a symbol for God, who is more than a Father and beyond complete knowing. At Pentecost the descent of the Holy Spirit is described in the words "tongues as of fire" (Acts 2:3), not a literal description but an effort to express something too big for words. The prophet Ezekiel frequently spoke in symbols because it was the best way he could communicate his experiences. He spoke of a vision: "And seated above the likeness of a throne was a likeness as it were of a human form" (Ezekiel 1:26b).

Children and symbolism

Margie was quite serious when she reported to her mother, "And she said that Nancy was crying her eyes out, but she wasn't, because I could see and her eyes were still there." Children are literal in their understanding.

"I don't want to be a sunbeam," sobbed Annette. "I'd rather be a child."

Children do not have this once-removed feeling about the world. Theirs is a life of direct, immediate participation. "A hole is for digging," expresses this attitude. A hole doesn't represent something that happened; it is something in itself. As they grow older, children begin to understand our odd adult way of talking, but not until they are in their teens. How can we expect children to get much out of phrases like "Ancient of days," "Shepherd of tender youth," "thou bright and morning star," all symbolic names for God?

What is the answer? Should we cut out all symbols, all symbolic language in dealing with children under twelve? How could we? Symbolism is so woven into the fabric of religious thinking and feeling and doing that it can not be divorced from religious teaching.

Symbolism affects feeling

Three-year-old Billy took his teacher on a tour of the church school rooms. When she did not hurry after him he grabbed her skirt and pulled her along in his eagerness to show her all the pictures. He didn't miss one. He pointed out all the pictures the children had drawn and displayed on the pin-up boards. "There's Jesus," he said of picture after picture, whether they were crude drawings done by small children or paintings by artists.

The teacher began to think about the way he always recognized Jesus. What was it? The faces of Jesus did not resemble each other; the situation was not always the same.

112

Perhaps it was the long white robe Jesus wore. Perhaps it was because Jesus was always the center of attention in the picture, even when there were other people in long robes with him. Jesus was the one adult shown with children; he was the one doing things, acts of power and love in healing people or feeding the crowds. To three-year-old Billy the long white robe, the person in the center doing acts of power and love, had become symbols by which he recognized Jesus. These symbols affected Billy's feelings rather than his verbal understanding. These were good, positive feelings clustering around the idea of Jesus.

On the other hand, unfavorable feelings can be attached to symbols. Miss Fenway remembers a round window, high up in the church she attended, which depicted an eye. Whether or not she was told this was the eye of God she does not remember, but she knows the feeling of fear that pervaded the church for her. She looked at the eye in the window and thought that this was the eye of God, always watching, never missing the smallest slip she might make. The symbol affected her feelings in such an unfavorable way that she disliked going to that church.

Symbols are of value in the child's religious experience because they affect his feelings and emotional tone. But they must be used wisely, with attention paid to the child's understanding, so that he will not get wrong understandings.

Symbols rightly used help the child to feel a part of the communion of saints, which is the church. They are so woven into the fabric of the life and thought of the church that the child cannot feel a part of this fellowship without using some of it's symbolism. Certain symbols are so important that the child needs to learn about them, such as the terms Shepherd, Lord, and King. Unless he understands something of their meaning, large areas of thought, in Bible and in hymns, are closed to him.

Symbolism also can help the child approach meanings. The use of "Father" as a name for God certainly helps children approach an understanding of one aspect of God's love as no amount of explaining will do. So we use symbols with children to enrich their worship and study. We will try to avoid using too many symbols, or symbols whose meaning the child cannot grasp, or those which are not essential to his Christian understanding. We must always guard against a symbol becoming more important than the reality.

The church building is a symbol

The child's first contact with religion beyond his home is the church. Here is a building set apart for worship, study, and fellowship, all with a particular group of people held together by their common loyalty to God. The very fact that there is such a building must influence a child's feeling about religion. If the building shows signs of being loved and cared for the child concludes that religion is important. If it is dirty and shabby when his home is clean and luxurious, he feels that religion is not important. Most churches are much larger than homes, with ceilings that look very high and faraway to the child. This impression of size and height influences his feelings, too.

The form of the church building is often symbolic. Some churches are built in the shape of a cross. Modern churches speak of a new appreciation of some aspects of our Christian faith. There is an effort to arrange the seating so that the worshiping congregation feels a sense of unity and belonging to the family of God. Often the chancel is not distinctly marked off from the nave of the church so that the worshiper will feel that in the Protestant tradition of the priesthood of believers the whole church is the chancel. One architect said he would like to build a church with one door to come in by and another door to go out by, so that worshipers would realize that the worship had changed them into different people.

The furniture of the church is symbolic. Protestant churches generally do not have a screen or curtain separating the worshiper from the altar. This direct access is a symbol of man's ability to turn directly to God, thanks to Jesus Christ. The altar is thought of primarily as a symbol of the table of the Lord, around which worshipers gather to participate in the Holy Communion with him. The central place given to the cross or crucifix reminds us of the centrality of redemption in our faith and experience. The candles on the altar may have been first used for the commonplace purpose of providing light, but they have come to signify to us Christ as the light of the world.

The classroom in which the children meet for study should also have its symbolic values. Does it speak to the child of the importance of Christian education? If it is a shabby room, contrasting with new public schools, bright libraries, fine recreation halls, luxurious homes, how can there be any doubt that it will symbolize to him a disregard for God? If the classroom is bright and cheerful, the child will also learn to feel that religion is cheerful.

Symbolic actions

When we salute the flag, or stand in the presence of people we wish to honor, or drink a toast to the bride and groom, we are performing symbolic actions. Religious life is full of them, too. Kneeling in humility for prayer, rising in reverence for the reading of the gospel, standing in witness as we say the Creed, these are all symbolic actions influencing our feelings and thoughts. When the pastor faces the altar in The Service, he symbolizes the fact that he is speaking on behalf of, or with, the congregation. When he faces the congregation he is acting out a symbol showing that he is bringing

God's Word to the people. When church councilmen stand before the altar to make their promises, their action is a symbol of dedication. Baptism, confirmation, the Lord's Supper—all these are solemn symbolic actions whereby we enlarge our understanding of God's ways with men. Children can learn much from these if they are explained at the right time.

People are symbols

"You know what I used to think," said Ricky confidentially. "I used to think that the pastor was God, especially when he stood in the pulpit and preached the sermon."

A surprising number of small children think of the pastor as God, and yet it should not be surprising to us since he is the one person they associate with the church and God's Word. He is always in the church when they are there, he takes the leading role in The Service, and during The Service he wears clothes unlike those of other people. The vestments of the pastor are symbolic of our tie with the past, for the cassock and surplice were the everyday clothes of men in the Roman Empire. As late as the sixth century these were ordinary clothes for clergy and laymen, the only distinction being that the clerical clothes worn for church services were particularly clean and finer than ordinary. In the Lutheran church of today the stole worn around the neck is a symbol that the wearer has been ordained to the ministry.

Just as the pastor is a symbol to the child, so too is the teacher. The teacher symbolizes the church and religion.

In William Golding's novel *Free Fall*, we see some English children in a classroom, listening to Miss Massey tell them Bible stories. All are listening except Johnny, whose mind is faraway in the clouds, flying an airplane. Disaster lands on Johnny.

" 'Why did I tell you those three stories?'

"Johnny mutters, 'I dunno miss.'

"Miss Massey hit him on both sides of the head, precisely with either hand, a word and a blow.

" 'God—'

"Smack!

" '—is—'

"Smack!

" '—love'

"Smack! Smack! Smack!"[5]

You know what Johnny learned about God. Far more important than the words, were the actions of Miss Massey. They were symbols of something. To Johnny, God was like Miss Massey.

The child builds up his ideas and feelings by many experiences and many symbols, but who we are and how we act as teachers influence his final decisions.

Words are symbols

Words are symbols. The word "c-h-u-r-c-h" does not look anything like the object it represents, but it stands for it. All words are symbols, but we are thinking here of special words that the Christian uses to stand for the great ideas of his religion—words which carry much more power than their literal meaning warrants. "Shepherd" is such a word. A shepherd one who cares for sheep, but in the Christian vocabulary it has become a picture of the loving care of the heavenly Father and the selfless devotion of Jesus Christ for his followers. How compelling this symbol is, can be deduced from the number of times it is used in the Bible, both in the Old Testament and the New Testament, and in the hymns of the church. It is a picture that was familiar to the people to whom Jesus spoke.

[5] William Golding, *Free Fall* (New York: Harcourt, Brace, and World, 1959).

To modern children "Shepherd" is a strange, unfamiliar symbol. They do not know shepherds; many of them have never seen a sheep. Even children growing up in the country are not familiar with the shepherd's care because our sheep are kept in fenced-in pastures and do not need a shepherd. But because the idea is so often used, because it expresses so well an important idea about God, it is worth the time we spend to explain it to children.

Sometimes symbols change in meaning. We are familiar with the word "king," but it does not mean to us what it meant to people in Paul's day, or in Martin Luther's day. To these long-ago people a king was a person with real power. He ruled over his kingdom with unlimited authority. There was an aura of divinity about him. Romans and Greeks felt that the king was semi-divine, and even Englishmen of Shakespeare's day felt that a king ruled as a representative of God and was on the throne by virtue of God's decree. Our children know of kings as characters in fairy tales, or as winners of popularity contests in the local high school, or as ceremonial figureheads of a state whose power is limited by elected officials.

In the same way the word "Lord" has been drained of its power because we do not know people who possess the authority of a lord in Bible times. In feudal times a lord not only ruled with real power, but he was also responsible for his vassals; he defended them against the depredations of others. There was a mutual loyalty demanded of lord and his man. This whole feeling has faded from our life. To whom do we owe obedience? Only to elected officials whose hold on office depends on our vote, or to a boss whose employ we can leave or against whom we can strike, or to a father who does not demand obedience but receives it as a matter of affection. It is not that we are free, but that we do not feel our lives to be at the mercy of a lord. Perhaps a difficulty in

Christian education is that we lack a symbol which will represent to the children the right of God to demand our obedience, the right of Jesus to expect our loyalty.

Stories are symbols

When Jesus said, "The kingdom of heaven is like . . ." he was presenting us with symbols that would tell us about the kingdom because it was the best way for us to understand. The kingdom is so different from our experience, so beyond our knowledge, that he had no way of giving us direct understanding. He could only tell us it was like a treasure hidden in a field, a merchant seeking pearls, a net gathering all kinds of fish from the sea. One value of a story as a symbol is that we can remember the story before we fully understand its meaning, and the story grows in significance as we bring enlarging experience to its interpretation.

119

Common symbols

All this talk about symbols before we come to the most common—the Alpha and Omega embroidered on the paraments, the sheaf of wheat, the grapevine in the church window! Symbols like these are packed with meaning; they are not mere decorations carved in the woodwork or embroidered on cloth.

Some symbols are easy to understand on the surface. In our own life we are familiar with water, or bread, or light, or a door. The child can understand that Jesus said he was the bread of life, the living Water, the light of the world, as a way of saying he was as necessary a part of our lives as light and bread and water. He understands the symbol on this elementary level, but it will be a long time before he gets more than that out of it.

Most of the symbols of the church are mysterious to the child and need some explanation before he can understand them at any level. We have referred to the symbol of the Shepherd, important in the thought and life of the church but strange to the child because it comes from an alien environment. In the same way the symbol of the vine is a powerful one, but it must be explained to many of our children who have never seen grapes growing on a vine. These rural symbols have power for those fortunate enough to have grown up in the country, but they only bewilder the urban or suburban child of today.

Other symbols need explanation because they come from other lands or other cultures. The lotus is a beautiful symbol that means much to Christians of India or Egypt. To us it needs explanation.

The whole group of symbols in Greek letters need explanation. Alpha and Omega are like A and Z. We say "from A to Z" to denote the complete gamut. Chi Rho are the equivalent of Ch and R, the first letters of the name "Christ." The early Christians used these letters to indicate the name of Christ.

In the days of the Roman Empire when it was dangerous to be a Christian, believers developed a secret sign by which they could communicate with other Christians. As two men stood talking the one might draw the outline of a fish in the sand or on the wall. If the second man were a Christian, he would recognize the first as a fellow Christian. The fish was their sign. Why? The word for fish in the Greek language was I-CH-TH-U-S. These letters were the first letters of a phrase "Iesous (Jesus)-CHristos (Christ)-THeou (of God)-Uios (son)-Soter (savior)."

Fifth- and sixth-graders find this story fascinating for the picture it gives of the early Christians as well as for the charm of passwords and mystery. For them the symbol can be explained and have meaning. Younger children would only be bewildered.

Some symbols use understandable objects, but their religious significance is not seen until explained. A symbol of the church is a ship. The child is familiar with a ship, but its claim to represent the church must be explained to him. The picture is that of a ship tossed about on stormy waters but secure in its voyage as the church has been tossed about by persecution and hardship but is still secure. The symbol calls to mind the story of Jesus in the ship with the disciples, quieting the stormy waters.

The symbols connected with the apostles are often familiar objects, but they have no symbolic meaning until their connection with the apostle is explained. Peter's symbol is keys, referring to Matthew 16:18-19.

Matthew has the symbol of money bags, reminding us that he had been a collector of taxes. Jude is symbolized by a sailboat because of the tradition that he made long missionary journeys over the seas. Keys, money bags, sailboats are

121

familiar objects, but their meaning as symbols depends on association and must be explained.

How shall we use symbols?

How, then, shall we make the best use of symbolism with children? On the one hand, the child does not understand the usual adult use of symbols. On the other hand, symbolism is woven into the fabric of our religious life. What shall we do?

1. Use the symbols that have power for the child, power to influence his feelings toward a greater appreciation of religion to help him approach the meaning of the mysteries that remain in our faith.

2. Explain symbols that he will meet in his church life, such as the cross and the candles on the altar, the pastor's turning to the altar, the symbolic phrases in the hymns he sings. "We stand or kneel to pray to show that we are in the presence of someone we love and honor more than anyone else." "The Shepherd cares for his sheep. He protects them from danger. He would die to keep them safe."

3. Do not burden the child with symbols he does not appreciate. Do not try to explain too many. Use them sparingly. Curb your own interest if symbols fascinate you, and do not try to impose that interest on the child.

THINGS WE SEE

Pictures

Glen came running into the room, then stopped short.

"That's different," he said, going close to the wall to examine the single picture Miss Schall had centered on the pin-up board, a Japanese picture of Christ. He studied it for a minute. "I never thought about that," he said to himself.

"Do you like the picture?" Miss Schall asked.

"I guess so. I never thought about it before, but I guess a Japanese painter would like to think of Jesus as Japanese. Why don't we use this picture during worship time? It helps you remember that—well, that Jesus isn't just for us."

Sometimes a picture can convey a message better than many words. As Glenn looked at this one he was first of all startled, because the idea of Jesus looking Japanese was strange. Then he realized that the Japanese artist was interpreting a Christian truth rather than giving a photographic likeness of Jesus, that the picture was saying Jesus was for all men. It helped Glenn to think of himself as one of a world-wide fellowship of followers of Jesus. When the group met for worship the picture strengthened the message of their hymn, their Scripture, and their prayer, all of which revolved around the theme of Jesus as the world's Savior.

Pictures can be used to create an atmosphere. Miss Friend's class found picture after picture of flowers and springlike scenes on the browsing table. As they pinned a number of them on the walls of their room, they began to think of the loveliness of springtime. They were ready for the mood of the day's worship time which was one of thankfulness to God, the Maker of the beauty of spring.

Mrs. Rhodes' third-graders had been making pictures of the story of the paralyzed man whose friends brought him to Jesus. Their pictures showed different scenes in the story: Jesus preaching to a crowd of people in the house, the four friends with the paralytic outside the house, the friends on the house roof, the friends letting the paralytic down through the uncovered roof, Jesus healing. During worship, the story was read and the pictures illustrating the story were held up. A deeper impression was made on the children than if they had heard the story by itself.

Sometimes children do not really notice permanently hung pictures because they have grown used to them. If you have several good pictures, display them one at a time and change them to fit the season or your worship ideas. You can gather a wealth of pictures for use from magazines, church bulletins, and Christmas cards. If you keep your pictures in a file, you will have available pictures that will help in worship.

Films and filmstrips

We have been thinking of pictures as those which hang on the wall or repose in a file. There is also a treasury of picture material in filmstrip and slides. The advantage of the pictures in a file is that they are inexpensive, available, and easily used. The advantage of a projected picture is that a whole group can look at it together. Filmstrips are arranged to present a series of related pictures to tell a story.

One disadvantage of projected pictures, however, is that the child has no part in selecting or using them. The machinery is cumbersome and requires an adult familiar with the technique. Also, our own attitude presents a problem; we are tempted to think of projected pictures as entertainment, or to use them with too little preparation, or to let the child look at them passively. Filmstrips will accomplish some things better than still pictures, but at the cost of more time and preparation. If you think of using filmstrips as a way out of teaching, or as an easier way, then you are not using them properly. Projected pictures should be used with children only when they are the best means of accomplishing your purpose and when their preparation and use does not take more time and effort than the results are worth.

Here are some suggestions about filmstrips:

Choose wisely. Look at a number of films to see which will best tell the story or present the points you have in mind. Ask yourself, "Will this filmstrip accomplish what I want? Is it the best way to do it? Would pictures from my file be just as good? Would some pupil activity (drawing, dramatizing) do the job better? How can I be sure that the children will be involved and not just sit there, passive, without thinking or reacting to what they see?"

Always preview the pictures. If a record accompanies the film, listen to it. Will your children understand it? Does it tell the story you want? Will it be best to use the filmstrip and record straight through? Or would your purpose be achieved by using part of the filmstrip? Would it be better to show the pictures and comment on them, or to tell the story yourself?

Make sure your equipment will work. Many filmstrips have been a waste of time because the projector wasn't ready or the record didn't play.

Preface the showing by telling the children what the filmstrip is about. Suggest things they may watch for.

Discussion about the story should follow the showing. Turn to any pictures which were not understood, or which arouse discussion, or which need to be emphasized.

Pictures, projected or not, can accomplish many things in worship instruction. In worship they can be used to tell a Bible story, to enrich our appreciation of parts of the Bible, to influence an atmosphere, to work out special programs, to instruct in worship, to give background information about hymns, and to give information about certain phases of worship.

The many possible uses of pictures do not mean that we are to embark on a wild orgy of using projector and picture file. They should be used when they are clearly the best way to achieve your objectives, but never as a crutch, or a cover-up for inadequate planning, or to fill time. Generally speaking, you will achieve more with children if you use pictures they have drawn themselves or have selected from an assortment on the browsing table, and then discuss the meaning and implication of the pictures they picked out.

The room in which you meet

When Mrs. Skinner, the new teacher, saw the room in which the first-graders met, her heart sank. The walls were a peculiar no-color, with suggestions of gray and tan and purple, all clouded over with grime and soot. The floor was a brownish red. Limp strips of cloth hung at the windows, as if someone, a lone time ago, had cared enough to put up curtains. The chairs did not match in size or color, although years of hard wear had knocked most of the paint off them so that you could scarcely see any color.

"If this room depresses the children as much as it does me," thought Mrs. Skinner, "and I know it does—it's going to be quite a job to help them rejoice because God's world is so beautiful!"

Mrs. Skinner did what she could. The next time she came she brought a bouquet of yellow daffodils. That helped. She asked several of the mothers to help her make new curtains for the windows. When they came to put them up the mothers realized how drab and dirty the room looked, so they enlisted their husbands in a painting project. Before they were through the walls had been painted a sunny yellow, the chairs were repaired and painted green, and the floor was a deeper shade of green. Mrs. Skinner watched as the children came into the refurbished room.

"Look," said Carol. "It's sunshiny in here now!"

When the opportunity came, Bruce said, "Thank you, God, for sunshine and grass and our new room."

Mrs. Skinner noted several effects. She found it easier to teach; the children seemed more co-operative and less restless and quarrelsome. They were more relaxed during worship and more receptive to suggestions about thanking God. She is convinced that the appearance of the room in which she teaches is one of the resources in worship.

Objects in the room can help create a worshipful mood, or

direct thoughts to a particular phase of worship. Flowers add color and brightness and provide a starting point for thoughts of gratitude to God for his beautiful world. A beautiful brass tray from India guided some fifth-graders into thoughts of concern for people of that country which they expressed in their prayers of intercession. Picture books about the stars helped Bobby and Bill to think about God's great universe and prepared them for worship.

THINGS WE HEAR

"Something's gone wrong with our connection," said the radio announcer. We'll have the baseball game for you in just a moment now." There was a moment of silence. Then the announcer's agitated voice. "Still no word from the field. While we're waiting I'll run over the results of the other games." The listener had the feeling that a great tragedy had taken place. The audience was threatened with several minutes of silence! This must be averted at all costs, by aimless talking, or recorded music, or anything except silence!

Sometimes we in the church seem to be just as afraid of stillness. Silence is not empty; it can speak to us of the presence of God in a way that makes words seem to interrupt.

Miss Madden was leading her children in worship. "Let's each one of us pray to God," she said. "We don't need to say any words. We'll just think about how thankful we are to our heavenly Father."

Heads were bowed and the room grew silent. After what seemed like a long time, Miss Madden said, "And we thank you for your love. Amen."

Heads came up. "I like praying like that," said Judy. "I had time to think."

There are other times when listening together to the music of a hymn played softly, or to recorded music, can be the gateway to worship. Like projected pictures, recordings should be used with discretion, and only when you feel that the record can achieve your objectives better than other methods.

Sometimes worship can be enriched by the use of wisely selected poems, stories, or written prayers. To a group that has been learning about the work of the church in Africa, hearing the right story from Africa may add new depths of feeling. Or using a prayer written by an African Christian may enhance the knowledge that we are all in one church.

But listening to poems or stories or prayers has value only when these writings are used to deepen or enrich the unity of the worship-learning situation. The time for introducing material of this kind is in the study session, when the necessary explanation and discussion can take place, not during the time of worship.

THINGS WE DO

The situation of our bodies can influence worship. Standing, kneeling, sitting relaxed, bowing our heads, closing our eyes—each of these actions can help to produce a desired mood.

1. *Activities.*

Activities can lead to the desire for worship. The fourth-graders made devotional guides for family use. When they were working on them Craig said, "Maybe we ought to pray for our families today."

The vacation church school study had been about the wonderful works of God in nature. Each junior had brought to class some object that illustrated this theme. Nancy came with flowers from the garden. Don brought an empty robin's egg. Gilly carried in her book about the stars. Jim had the ant colony he had been given for his birthday. The class talked about these various signs of God's creation. As they planned their worship these boys and girls had so many ideas they could not use them all. They thought of psalms that told about God's world, about hymns that sang God's praises, of prayers that expressed delight and wonder in all that God had done.

Tim and Stan had been loud in their lack of interest in anything the group was doing. No, they didn't want to do this. No, that was a dud. Then, to Miss Allen's surprise, the boys became interested in the large picture map of India, which was a suggested project. They worked at it industriously, coloring sections, cutting out the extra pictures, reading the information with it. They explained it so well to the rest of the group that the class decided they would like to do something to help people in India. The activity had given the class a real motivation for service of some kind.

Sometimes activity is a result of worship and gives expression to the desire to share or helps the child carry out resolves he has made. In the worship time Miss Spencer's children had prayed for people in hospitals and for old people. The prayers had been heartfelt. Now they wanted to express their concern in doing something for the older people. They decided to buy a plant for old Mrs. Reynolds, who lived near the church, and take it to her. The worship experience was more satisfying because it was followed by a way the children could do something for the person for whom they had prayed.

One kind of activity that has special value in worship is writing prayers, collects, litanies, and psalms.

Lennie, writing a sentence prayer in his vacation church school workbook, thought about his reasons for thanking God as he had never thought before. When the prayer was written, "Thank you, God, for all the fun in the world," Lennie had taken a big step toward relating God to all that he does and is. When a group works out a litany of praise, they are thinking together about the very basis of worship. If these prayers and litanies are used, the children recognize that worship is something that concerns them, not something they do in imitation of adults.

2. *The child's own experiences.*

Sometimes we overlook the resources at hand in the child's own life. He goes to church, he goes to school, he plays with others, he sees TV programs. All this experience and information can enrich his worship and be related to it. The teacher can draw on the child's everyday experiences to help him understand the meaning of wrongdoing and penitence, of forgiveness, of loyalty and devotion, so that he can express these in his worship. The teacher can help the child to see that his daily living affects his relationship with God. He can help the child find ways to put his resolutions and dedications to work, ways in which his impulses to share can bear fruit.

3. *Church life.*

The child gains strength and understanding from his membership in the communion of the church. All his experiences of worship in the classroom, whether spontaneous or planned, should be undergirded by the corporate life of the church. The awareness that he belongs to a fellowship of those who believe in Jesus Christ should aid his Christian growth. Not only should the child know that he belongs to this fellowship, but the members of the church should feel a sense of responsibility for the inclusion of the child. The child should be remembered in prayer by adult believers; his welfare should be a part of all church planning.

The children should be included not only in festive occasions but in almost all church activities. If the church is engaged in a building campaign, children should share the interest and enthusiasm and be given an opportunity to support it. If the church is engaged in evangelism, children should share the concern for those outside the church. We cannot raise children to enjoy the fullest possible life of worship unless they are made to feel that they are members of the whole church, with its great strength and power to support them and its great enterprises demanding their sharing and devotion.

PEOPLE

"Wouldn't it be nice to have Pastor Grant worship with us," Miss Leonard suggested. "But he is so busy I don't like to ask him."

But she did, with many apologies, and the pastor replied, "Of course, I have time to visit your children and join their worship. I can think of no more important task in the church."

The pastor is a worshipful resource indeed, for he represents the church to children as no other person does. Very likely he has spent more time and study in thinking about worship than anyone else in the church. While all members of a church must share the pastor's time, the children have a right to their share and the pastor will be happy to give it to them.

The musicians of the church can be resource people, too. On occasion they may help you with the music, or help to instruct the children in the musical parts of worship. Often they will be glad to talk with you and give you advice or materials to help in your work. Directors of Christian education, members of the Christian education committee, church councilmen, and many others can be helpful.

All these resources may be used in the compelling task of helping children to worship, but the one which will have the most influence is you. Your own attitude toward worship and your own rich experiences in worship will influence the children far more than you suspect. Even though much that you say about worship will be forgotten, the children you teach will remember the tone of your voice, the expression on your face—all the countless intangible witnesses of the worship life you lead. In your own personal worship, at home or in church, you may sometimes feel that you are only going through the motions. But this feeling has been the experience of most Christians. Increasingly your worship will be rich and full, and as this happens, the children you lead, will grow closer to God because you are closer to him. And their love and loyalty to their Lord will inspire you, in turn.

Helping children worship is a wonderful thing. Jesus' twin commandments were that we love God with all our heart and soul and mind and our neighbors as ourselves. These we fulfill as we worship together.

"Thou rising morn in praise rejoice"

Patsy Douglass—Grade 6

APPENDIXES

Appendix A

Objectives for Growth in Worship

AGE ONE
To share in family worship at least by posture and quietness and to learn actions such as folded hands and bowed head which will later become meaningful to the pupil.

AGE TWO
To begin to recognize singing and praying as elements of worship and to sing simple songs and pray simple prayers.

AGE THREE
To learn to worship happily with friends in church school; to learn to tell God things in prayer and to express thanks and praise in song.

AGE FOUR
To participate more fully in the worship of family and church schools; to deepen his reverence for God; to associate the Bible with worship activities; to learn to worship and pray spontaneously and creatively at many times.

AGE FIVE
To learn new worship forms and to participate more meaningfully in them; to learn to pray in Jesus' name; to deepen respect for the church as God's house and to identify church with people who go to the church building for worship, learning, etc.

AGE SIX
To develop habits of regular attendance and participation at church and church school; to become better acquainted with the heritage of patterns of worship (hymns, prayers, use of Bible); to assume more personal responsibility for participating in worship at home and at church.

AGE SEVEN

To participate in church worship as well as worship in church school; to express love and appreciation of God's gifts in nature through worship, drawing, music, etc.; to know certain Psalms as expressions of praise.

AGE EIGHT

To begin to express in confession to God his sorrow for sin; to help plan worship in church school; to strengthen the habit of regular attendance at church and its schools.

AGE NINE

To enrich his personal devotional life; to participate in the church liturgy with greater understanding; to know more hymns of the church; to have a sense of awe before a holy God.

AGE TEN

To compose written prayers and help plan worship services; to sense the need of prayer in his life more fully; to worship in church with true joy and responsiveness.

AGE ELEVEN

To know the meaning of familiar church symbols; to use his talents (e.g., singing) in church services; to use the Bible creatively in worship.

AGE TWELVE

To develop a more mature relationship to God in prayer and worship; to appreciate God's speaking to him through prayer; to appreciate elements of prayer such as adoration, confession, thanksgiving, intercession and petition; to express gratitude to God through worship; to recognize prayer as a channel for the activity of the Holy Spirit; to expand his knowledge of great hymns, symbolism, art; to be better able to lead group worship.

AGE THIRTEEN

To gain a deeper understanding of the church liturgies; to worship with enthusiasm and interest; to gain a growing wonder, awe and reverence for God's power and wisdom in creation.

AGE FOURTEEN

To appreciate the witness of the gospel in music, art, architecture, literature, etc.; to know and use more classical liturgical prayers in life situations; to express his faith through the art forms of the church such as drama, music, painting, and choral speech.

AGE FIFTEEN

To gain a more mature understanding of prayer; to participate intelligently in private and corporate worship; to strengthen habits of church attendance, use of sacraments, daily Bible reading, etc.

Appendix B

A Brief Explanation of The Service

<table>
<tr><td>OUTLINE</td><td>EXPLANATION</td></tr>
</table>

I. WE CONFESS OUR SINS

The Invocation
("In the name of . . .")

We invoke the presence of the Triune God upon our worship in a scriptural formula which summarizes what we know of God. Matthew 28:19.

Exhortation
("Beloved in the Lord")

A reminder that access to God is possible through Jesus Christ, and encouragement to "draw near." Hebrews 10:22; John 1:8f.

Versicles and Responses
("Our help . . ."
"I said, I will
confess . . .")

Mutual encouragement of pastor and people upon scriptural grounds of forgiveness. Psalm 124:8; Psalm 32:5.

Confession of Sins
("Almighty God, our
Maker")

The minister confesses (1) original sin, (2) actual sin, and (3) helplessness of himself and his people.

Prayer for Grace
("O Most Merciful God")

Congregation joins minister in prayer for mercy, forgiveness, spiritual knowledge and obedience, everlasting life.

Declaration of Grace
("Almighty God, our . . .")

Pastor's pronouncement of God's mercy and forgiveness to those who believe in him. John 1:12, 3:16; Mark 16:16.

138

II. WE GIVE PRAISE

The Introit for the Day

Actual beginning of The Service. "Introit" means entrance, is a fragment from the Psalms announcing the theme of the day. Entire Introit psalm was used originally. Begins the "Variable" part of The Service.

The Gloria Patri
("Glory be to the Father")

An ancient hymn of praise to the Triune God. It distinguishes the Christian use of the psalter and connects Old Testament texts with the later and fuller revelation of the New Testament. Romans 16:27; Ephesians 3:21; Philippians 4:20.

The Kyrie
("Lord, have mercy . . .")

A responsive prayer of intercession used in fourth century Jerusalem in the Liturgy of St. James.

The Gloria in Excelsis
("Glory be to God on high")

Ancient hymn of praise based on the angels' song at Jesus' birth, Luke 2:14.

III. WE RECEIVE GOD'S WORD

Salutation and Response
("The Lord be with you")

Pastor and people pray mutually for each other. Ruth 2:4; Judges 6:12; Luke 1:28; 2 Thessalonians 3:16; 2 Timothy 4:22.

The Collect for the Day

A brief, formal prayer which "collects" and concentrates the thoughts of the day (epistle and gospel) and prepares the heart for the Word to be read. Usual parts: invocation, reason, petition, purpose, ending.

The Lesson	First of the liturgical lessons; from the Old Testament.
The Epistle	A selection, usually from the New Testament Epistles (letters) contributing to the theme of the day.
Gradual for the Day	A psalm fragment echoing the thought for the day, and connecting epistle and gospel. Gradual means "step."
Alternatives: "The Hallelujah"	The Old Testament cry "Praise the Lord." Music from Palestrina, arranged by Monk, Cf. Hymn 90.
Sentence for the Season	The theme of the season in song.
The Gospel for the Day	The central Scripture lesson for the day, from Jesus' own words and teachings. We stand to honor Christ.
The Apostles' or Nicene Creed	Ancient formula of the faith, developed from the baptismal confession and giving concise summary of Christian doctrine. Expresses our acceptance of the Word just read. Sum of Christian doctrine, elaborating the deity of Jesus Christ. Formulated at Council of Nicea, A.D. 325. Used on festivals and at Communion.
The Hymn	The principal hymn of The Service, to relate to lessons of the day and help prepare for the sermon.
The Sermon	E x p o s i t i o n, proclamation, and preaching of the Word applied to spiritual needs of man.
The Votum ("The peace of God . . .")	A fitting benediction following the sermon. Philippians 4:7.

IV. WE GIVE OUR OFFERING

The Offertory	A psalm-prayer of consecration. Psalm 51:17-19; Psalm 116:12-13, 18-19; Psalm 51:10-12.
The Offering	An act of worship and expression of our stewardship. We present gifts for support of the church.
The Prayer of the Church	Prayer of the whole church for the needs of all mankind.
The Lord's Prayer	The "Model Prayer," an all-inclusive and fitting conclusion to the General Prayer.
The Hymn	Concluding expression of prayer, praise and/or thanksgiving; or if Holy Communion is to follow, a preparation for the Communion Service.

V. WE RECEIVE GOD'S GIFT

The Preface Salutation and Response Sursum Corda and Exhortation Vere Dignum	Solemn preparation for what is to follow. Mutual prayer for pastor and people. "Lift up your hearts." "It is truly meet . . ." The eucharistic prayer of thanksgiving with proper preface for the season.
The Sanctus: "Holy, Holy, Holy"	Concludes the Preface. Isaiah 6:2-3; Psalm 118; Matthew 21:9.
The Prayer of Thanksgiving	An appropriate prayer widely used in Christian worship, incorporating the Words of Institution.
The Lord's Prayer	Following contemporary European practice, the conclusion is a response by the people.

141

The Pax
("The peace of the Lord . . .")

A sacramental announcement of the gift of peace promised by Christ to his disciples, John 20:19-21. Luther: "It is the voice of the Gospel announcing the forgiveness of sins." A dignified blessing of the people.

The Agnus Dei
("O Christ, Thou Lamb of God")

An ancient communion hymn of devotion, from A.D. 700. Based on John 1:29.

The Administration

The worshipers receive the Sacrament of the Real Presence in faith and devout love.

The Nunc Dimittis

Expresses fullness of spiritual satisfaction and the personal appropriation of God's gifts of salvation. The song of Simeon, Luke 2:29-32. Begins "The Post-Communion."

The Thanksgiving

Prayers of gratitude and joy, with emphasis on the Sacrament as God's gift to man, not an offering of man to God.

The Salutation and Benedicamus
("The Lord be with you . . ."
"Bless we the Lord . . .")

These introduce the benediction. "Bless we the Lord" is a doxology which concludes each of the five books of the psalter, Psalms 41, 72, 89, 106, 150. Therefore, an appropriate conclusion to the Christian liturgy.

The Benediction

The imparting of God's blessing to the worshiping congregation. God's command to Moses, Numbers 6:22-27. Also Christ's final act with his disciples, Luke 24:50. (The New Testament benediction, used elsewhere, is from 2 Corinthians 13:14.)

142

Type: Body, 11 on 13 and 10 on 11 Caledonia
Display, Sansura
Paper: White Test Offset